KNAVES AND SWINDLERS

Essays on the Picaresque Novel in Europe

UNIVERSITY OF HULL PUBLICATIONS

Knaves
and Swindlers

ESSAYS ON THE
PICARESQUE NOVEL IN EUROPE

EDITED BY
CHRISTINE J. WHITBOURN

Published for the UNIVERSITY OF HULL *by*
OXFORD UNIVERSITY PRESS
LONDON   NEW YORK   TORONTO
1974

Oxford University Press, Ely House, London W.1

GLASGOW   NEW YORK   TORONTO   MELBOURNE   WELLINGTON
CAPE TOWN   IBADAN   NAIROBI   DAR ES SALAAM   LUSAKA   ADDIS ABABA
DELHI   BOMBAY   CALCUTTA   MADRAS   KARACHI   LAHORE   DACCA
KUALA LUMPUR   SINGAPORE   HONG KONG   TOKYO

ISBN 0 19 713420 3

*Printed in Great Britain
by W & J Mackay Limited, Chatham*

CONTENTS

The editor wishes to thank very warmly all those who have helped in the production of this book and, in particular, her five fellow-contributors, whose consistent kindness and consideration have made comparatively easy the difficult task of editorship.

LIST OF ABBREVIATIONS

AN SSSR	Akademiya Nauk Soyuza Sovetskikh Sotsialisticheskikh Respublik (Academy of Sciences of the Union of Soviet Socialist Republics)
BH	*Bulletin Hispanique*
BHS	*Bulletin of Hispanic Studies*
CL	*Comparative Literature*
ECr	*Essays in Criticism*
Fi	*Filología*
FMLS	*Forum for Modern Language Studies*
GLL	*German Life and Letters*
GQ	*German Quarterly*
GR	*Germanic Review*
HispI	*Hispanófila*
HR	*Hispanic Review*
Ib	*Iberoromania*
KFLQ	*Kentucky Foreign Language Quarterly*
KRQ	*Kentucky Romance Quarterly*
MLQ	*Modern Language Quarterly*
MLR	*Modern Language Review*
NRFH	*Nueva Revista de Filología Hispánica*
PMLA	*Publications of the Modern Language Association of America*
PQ	*The Philological Quarterly*
RF	*Romanische Forschungen*
RFE	*Revista de Filología Española*
RHisp	*Revue Hispanique*
RO	*Revista de Occidente*
RoN	*Romance Notes*
RR	*Romanic Review*
SlRev	*Slavonic and East European Review*
SRev	*Slavic Review*

INTRODUCTION

During the session 1969–70 a course of lectures was arranged in the University of Hull in which members of several departments discussed the picaresque novel as it appeared in different European countries. At the end of the course a suggestion was made that these lectures might be turned into a joint publication, and this volume is the result. The lectures have in some cases been quite extensively revised, but their scope remains approximately the same as when they were delivered, and it will be noticed that in some the conversational tone of the lecture has been preserved. As the form of the book was dictated largely by the content of the lectures, its range is necessarily rather restricted. In both English and Spanish, and no doubt in other European literatures also, there has been a modern flowering of the picaresque tradition which would have provided interesting points of comparison with the seventeenth and eighteenth-century novels, but our scope has not allowed us to draw such comparisons. We have confined ourselves to those novels which, if they have not arisen directly as a result of the seventeenth-century Spanish tradition, at least have strong affinities with it. The characteristics of this tradition will already be well known: the low birth and disreputable background of the protagonists; their attempts to gain themselves a living by begging, deception and petty theft; the absence of a romantic love interest and the feeling that love and marriage are a snare; the episodic technique, in which the protagonist creates the chief link between a series of adventures; the everyday and contemporary setting; the corruption of a young person by a deceitful world; the questioning of accepted values through a persistently ambiguous attitude.

It seemed to those of us who participated in the course that comparative studies of the picaresque tradition can be very illuminating, and that a composite work of this kind could be of interest to students in a variety of fields. The various comparative studies

so far produced have usually been the work of a single author, and
therefore inclined to be weighted towards the area of his specializa-
tion. Even if a formal balance is maintained, the value of the
critical judgments is often uneven. This book, with its series of
specialist studies conveniently gathered together in one volume,
represents a different kind of comparative study from those referred
to above, and one which we hope will prove useful to students of
the tradition. The juxtaposition of the essays will enable the reader
to make his own comparisons, but it may perhaps be helpful to
indicate some of the different patterns of development represented
by the works discussed.

Mateo Alemán's *Guzmán de Alfarache* being, if one regards
Lazarillo de Tormes as something of a precursor of the genre, the
earliest of the picaresque novels, was also the most influential,
since it established the form and influenced subsequent Spanish
writers as well as foreign ones. J. A. Jones's study demonstrates
that the work embodies that ambiguous attitude which I regard
as an important and characteristic feature of the mainstream of the
Spanish picaresque tradition and to which I have devoted a separate
essay. The meaning and the structure of *Guzmán* have been a
subject of controversy almost since the first appearance of the
novel, some maintaining that it is an illustration of the doctrine of
Original Sin, in which redemption is finally brought about by the
repentance of the sinner and the consequent gift of Divine Grace,
while others have seen it as a fundamentally pessimistic work, in
which the protagonist, whether because unable or unwilling to
pursue a virtuous life, persists in sin. Jones argues that Alemán, by
creating a character whose behaviour was consistent in these two
quite different contexts, has produced a work which is capable of
interpretation at more than one level and which has greater depth
and significance as a result.

The subtlety and depth of Alemán's work is interestingly
brought home by a consideration of the work of two of his translators, in Germany and France. Professor Parker discusses the
translation by Aegidius Albertinus published at Munich in 1615,
and uses the fact that Albertinus, who knew only the first part of
Guzmán, independently added a second part in which Guzmán is
brought to conversion and repentance as evidence that this would
be the natural outcome so far as the contemporary reader was

concerned: 'Albertinus's Second Part has scant literary merit, but it does demonstrate that it was natural in Counter-Reformation Europe to see the religious spirit and the religious direction that Alemán had given to his First Part.'[1] Albertinus, in fact, saw the conversion as inevitable and portrayed it in an unequivocal manner, and in this respect he was followed by Grimmelshausen.

Lesage, whose free translation of *Guzmán* was published in Paris in 1732, interpreted the work purely as a novel of delinquency, ignoring its religious message. The motive of revenge to which he ascribes Guzman's denunciation of his fellow galley-slaves is perfectly credible in view of the previous development of his character (he had, after all, taken revenge on his inhospitable relations in Genoa before leaving Italy), and the ending of the story is perfectly logical, though it may be more frivolous. It is not surprising to find that Alemán's moralizing digressions have disappeared, since these were not relevant to the theme of the book as conceived by Lesage and, as he ignored the spiritual message of Alemán's work, merely an unnecessary encumbrance. Lesage's own *Gil Blas*, while in places strongly reminiscent of *Guzmán*, also owes much to the more romanticized type of picaresque tale to which I refer in my subsequent essay.

Both the above interpretations are perfectly justifiable, but it is the skilful combination of them that makes Alemán's novel so interesting. The work may be seen as an illustration of the gulf that exists between man's perfectly sincere aspirations to virtue and his limited ability, when faced with temptation and need, to lead a virtuous life. The most difficult problems are those in which right and wrong are intermingled, and by presenting the reader with a work in which the moral distinctions are blurred and where some responsibility for interpretation rests with him, Alemán has produced a truer and fuller version of the problem of life than his two translators.

Consideration of Albertinus's translation brings one to the first really noteworthy imitator of the Spanish genre, Hans Jacob Christoffel von Grimmelshausen (1621?–76) who forms the subject of the essay by J. M. Ritchie. In *Der abenteuerliche Simplicissimus* Grimmelshausen preserves the unequivocal nature of the hero's

---

[1] A. A. Parker: *Literature and the Delinquent: The Picaresque Novel in Spain and Europe, 1599–1753* (Edinburgh 1967), p. 79.

conversion, following the German precedent of Albertinus. Ritchie points out that it was part of Grimmelshausen's aim to create an essentially *German* pícaro and the work has several features which are fundamentally different from its Spanish predecessors. One of these is the very strong emphasis on the corrupting influence of war. In the Spanish novels the background is normally one of civilian rather than military life and where it is not, as in *Estebanillo González*, war is more of a backcloth than an absolutely essential element, as it is in *Simplicissimus*. Just as *El buscón* is a study of the effect of heredity and environment on a young boy, so is *Simplicissimus* a study of the effect of war. Every incident is provoked by it, every temptation is the result of it, and when Simplicius goes to Switzerland on a pilgrimage with Herzbruder his instant response to a land at peace is deeply impressive. No Spanish novel integrates the theme of war so closely with the protagonist's development or treats it on so serious a plane.

Another noticeable difference between *Simplicissimus* and the Spanish novels is the presence in the former of a quite strong supernatural element—witches, devils, magic and prophecies. Simplicius becomes involved in a witches' orgy and is magically translated from Hirschfeld to Magdeburg; old Herzbruder has a gift of prophecy, and other prophecies which are subsequently fulfilled are also referred to; incomprehensible horrors and a supposed ghost accompany the treasure Simplicius discovers in an abandoned castle near Soest; a devil denounces Simplicius at Einsiedeln. Most important of all is the episode of the Mummelsee and the miraculous spring. All these elements are quite foreign to the Spanish picaresque novel, in which the background is very realistic, and events highly credible.[1] Any apparently miraculous occurrence usually turns out to be an elaborately contrived imposture. In *Simplicissimus* the problem of good and evil is worked out in accordance with a different tradition but with no less intensity and commitment than in *Guzmán*. Simplicius is also untypical in that his origins are noble, although he is unaware of this for a large part of the work. He ultimately adopts voluntarily the simple virtuous life his father has led before him; it is the tragedy of

---

[1] The events described in the 1555 continuation of *Lazarillo* are exceptional in this respect, and Juan de Luna, in his later (1620) continuation, comments scathingly on their absurdity.

Pablos *el buscón* that he cannot rise above *his* heredity.

A similar series of similarities and differences can be charted in connection with Grimmelshausen's other major picaresque work *Courasche*. Parker has pointed out a certain affinity with *El buscón*,[1] and it is certainly true that both protagonists sink lower and lower as the book proceeds and end in a state of unrepentant and degraded persistence in the picaresque life. The moral should be clear: both works portray a deplorable character whose career should under no circumstances be imitated. But just as the moral of *El buscón* is offset by one's sympathy for the weak protagonist who is the victim of his heredity and environment, so is the moral of *Courasche* offset by the admiration of the reader for the indomitable spirit of Courage herself. It is difficult to think of a character in any of the Spanish novels who is in any way comparable. Some *pícaras* display a certain degree of initiative and strength of character, but none can approach Courage in interest and complexity, or in the power to dominate. Courage is strong, positive, masterful—in every way, as Ritchie says, 'a magnificent beast'. The work starts with an outburst of mockery and defiance and ends with sentiments of contempt for the fools who allow themselves to be so easily duped and robbed. Courage is corrupted and degraded and entirely aware of her own degradation, but she does not sink under the weight of it; she flaunts it with resolute defiance. Her strength of character and her ability to get the better of any situation, coupled with her frankness and self-knowledge, inspire respect and with this respect, a reluctance to accept the moral at its face value. *Courasche* therefore reflects the ambiguity of the Spanish tradition in a way that *Simplicissimus* does not.

Grimmelshausen in seventeenth-century Germany concentrated upon the basic themes of virtue, vice and war; Lesage in eighteenth-century France was more preoccupied by considerations of elegance and entertainment. He transformed Alemán's work into an agreeable and entertaining novel while suppressing its deeper significance, and the attitude which characterizes his translation is also discernible in his own novel, *Gil Blas*. It makes pleasant reading, but does not attempt to deal with any basic human problem. Gil Blas is fundamentally honourable; where he is forced by circumstances into some dishonourable action it subsequently becomes a

---

[1] A. A. Parker: *Literature and the Delinquent*, p. 97.

matter of regret to him and he makes what amends he can, as in the case of his desertion of his parents and uncle. He, like Fielding's Tom Jones, is a young man on the threshold of life who lives for a period on his wits and who eventually settles down into middle-class respectability. Neither Gil Blas nor Tom Jones suffered the doubts and humiliations of Guzmán or Pablos. But although Lesage's novel may not have been remarkably original in its own right, both his own novel and his translations of Spanish novels were very popular, and he constitutes an important link between Spain and France and, indeed, between Spain and England, as his works were translated into English and became well known on both sides of the channel. Rather than bringing anything new to the genre, Lesage's contribution lay in the dissemination and popu-larization of the tradition, although his is the only French novel of interest which can really be said to correspond to the traditional picaresque form.

Other French writers, however, made use of picaresque elements in works of greater originality. One critic has referred to the 'ragged cloak of the cynical philosopher'[1] which envelops the *pícaro*, and two major French writers of the eighteenth century, Voltaire and Diderot, were quick to perceive the philosophical possibilities of the genre. Voltaire, whose *Candide* was published in 1759, parodied the picaresque novel in an attempt to demolish Leibniz's philosophy of optimism. Many of the traditional components of the novel are present: the episodic technique; the theft and deception (not on the part of Candide himself, but by those with whom he is from time to time associated), the protagonist's journey and flight from justice, the storms at sea, the capture by pirates, the unexpected reunion, the recital of life stories, the ultimate attainment of tranquillity. Many commonplaces of the tradition are incorporated, but the action is telescoped to an extraordinary extent, incident follows incident and horror follows horror with a rapidity which fascinates, while at the same time rendering the tale entirely fantastic. Candide begins life in Germany and, like Simplicius, he encounters the horrors of war while still entirely innocent, but there the similarity ends. Voltaire is not concerned, as was Grimmelshausen, with presenting a realistic and detailed account

[1] M. Romera Navarro: *Historia de la literatura española* (2nd edition, Boston 1949), p. 216.

of the dreadful nature of war and its effect upon a young man. He dismisses in a few lines the carnage, the raped women, the old men battered to death, the burning, ruins and brutality, and exploits the comic possibilities of Candide's naïve reactions and his persistent belief that all must be for the best in the best of all possible worlds. It is only the cumulative effect of a quite unbelievable series of horrors which finally forces Candide to compromise in his philosophy. The picaresque framework has here become a tool. It is subsidiary to the main aim, which is to argue a philosophical point of view. In fact Candide himself does not have any of the usual delinquent qualities of the picaresque protagonist. He is of noble (if illegitimate) birth and is known to be so from the outset, his mind occupies itself with the abstract rather than the material, and although he commits three murders in the course of the work, the treatment is such that the reader cannot regard them seriously. Candide's whole attitude is far from the petty thefts and deceptions which characterize the Spanish *pícaro*, but the form and conventions have been adapted in a new and interesting way to serve a philosophical end.

The French 'philosophization' of the picaresque genre is equally well exemplified by Diderot's *Le Neveu de Rameau*, which A. R. Strugnell has chosen as the subject of his study. In this case it is the figure of the *pícaro* himself that has been abstracted and used, rather than the form. The form used is the dialogue, traditionally a common vehicle for philosphical discussion, and at first sight the work has little in common with the picaresque genre. Strugnell, however, points out that *Le Neveu* incorporates the survey of society common in picaresque novels and that Rameau himself has many of the characteristics of the traditional *pícaro*. He does nevertheless differ from the conventional *pícaro* in one important respect —that he attempts to elevate his way of life to a philosophy. Other *pícaros* may live in the same way as Rameau, by parasitism and fraud, but their attempts at self-justification are along quite different lines; behind their delinquent activities lies a conventional morality. It is Rameau's apparent lack of any such morality which is so disturbing to the philosopher, and his extensive experience of the world which causes the philosopher to question his own values. The philosopher finds himself suddenly confronted with an organized system for living which his own morality tells him is wrong but which, because of his own lack of experience, he cannot adequately refute. Eventually he finds the weak point in his opponent's armour: in order to pursue his system to its logical conclusion Rameau should subordinate the last vestiges of integrity to his own self-interest, and this he finds himself unable to do. So the philosopher is vindicated, but not until his complacent morality has been given a severe jolt. The questioning of established moral and social values is a common characteristic of the picaresque novel and Rameau, who combines the most deplorable moral standards with a brilliant and colourful individuality, presents very eloquently the case for non-conformism. The work also continues the tradition of ambiguity, because the conflict between Rameau and the philosopher is not resolved in an unequivocal way. Strugnell shows how first one and then the other gains the upper hand, but neither emerges untouched from the encounter and neither is a clear victor. Each has been in some measure obliged to modify his opinions. Although form and treatment are in many respects quite foreign to the picaresque tradition (though one should not forget that both Cervantes's *Coloquio de los perros* and Alcalá Yáñez's *Alonso, mozo de muchos amos* (*Alonso, servant of many masters*) are dialogued), in others Diderot's work reflects the characteristics of the original Spanish novels more strongly than does Lesage's.

In Defoe's *Moll Flanders*, published in 1722 and here studied by J. A. Michie, the link with the Spanish tradition is more direct and apparent. Several of the Spanish novels had been translated into English (though sometimes with significant alterations) and had become extremely popular. Parker has pointed out that Moll's disreputable origin, her aspirations to gentility, and her gradual deterioration and eventual conversion are all characteristics for which parallels can be found in the Spanish tradition.[1] Whilst paying tribute to Defoe's apparently artless verisimilitude and to his humanitarianism, however, he finds the work deficient in that it fails to probe beneath the surface reality and establish a life pattern of depth and significance. Michie argues that Defoe is more preoccupied with such considerations than he has habitually been given credit for and regards it as one of his major achievements that he successfully imposes the deeper unity of an account of Moll's spiritual deterioration upon the surface unity of her apparent

[1] A. A. Parker: *Literature and the Delinquent*, pp. 102–3.

success story. Moll's narrative, he suggests, makes the most of the extenuating circumstances which surround her discreditable acts, but these circumstances do not absolve her of responsibility for her repeated moral compromises. She succeeds, but at a cost. Each new step into wrongdoing is accompanied by feelings of horror and revulsion, but these are soon overcome, and it is only in the last extremity that she shows any signs of true repentance. The suspect nature of her conversion is endorsed by the author's remarks in the preface, where she is described as living to a ripe old age, 'but was not so extraordinary a penitent as she was at first'.[1] Moll's previous behaviour makes it possible to believe in her conversion or not to believe in it: on the one hand her conduct is frequently reprehensible and dishonest, with an increasing tendency to harden in crime; on the other hand she does from time to time show herself to be capable of both virtue and loyalty, particularly when her social aspirations are for the time being satisfied. Defoe's novel presents yet another example of ambiguity in the picaresque tradition: if one doubts the permanence of Guzmán's conversion one may doubt that of Moll's; if Lazarillo achieved 'success' at the price of integrity, so does she.

From Diderot's *Neveu de Rameau,* written sometime between 1761 and 1784 and therefore the most recent of the works so far considered, to Gogol's *Dead Souls,* published in 1842, is a long gap. It represents a period, moreover, in which important advances had been made in novelistic technique. Nevertheless T. E. Little, in his study in this volume, points out that the work has significant affinities with the European picaresque tradition in spite of its obvious differences. Chichikov is a swindler, a flatterer and a physical coward; he is the principal link in a series of episodes in which he journeys from one place to another; he has the under-privileged background of the Spanish *pícaro,* he cultivates only those people who can be useful to him, and his aim is to attain an acceptable social and economic status. It is also apparent that the scheme of the work, of which Gogol completed only the first part, was designed to show not only Chichikov's life of petty crime and fraud, but also his subsequent repentance and redemption. Little points out that Gogol's technique of characterization is entirely unrealistic and that his preoccupations were moral rather

[1] *The Fortunes and Misfortunes of the Famous Moll Flanders* (London 1965), p. xi.

than social, and this view is endorsed by Gogol himself, who denied that his work was a picture of Russian provincial life or of Russian landowners. He regarded the first part of *Dead Souls* 'as a pale introduction to the great epic poem which is taking shape in my mind and which will finally solve the riddle of my existence'.[1] One can therefore detect in Gogol the same preoccupation with the problems of divine and human relationships, of good and evil, of sin and temptation, which are evident in *Simplicissimus* and *Guzmán de Alfarache*. Certain points of technique, however, instantly strike one as uncharacteristic of the picaresque form as exemplified by the Spanish novels and their immediate descendants. The number of episodes is far more restricted, and the characters who emerge from them are as interesting and as fully developed as the protagonist himself. In the earlier picaresque novels suspense was not normally sustained beyond the end of an episode; in *Dead Souls* some time elapses before the reader discovers the nature of Chichikov's business in the area, and it is not until towards the end of the novel that he is made fully aware of the reasons which lie behind it. A similar mystery surrounds Chichikov's origins, which are not revealed until the last chapter; in other novels in the tradition it is common for the life story to be treated in a strictly chronological manner.

How far Gogol was influenced by the European picaresque tradition is difficult to determine. The tradition became known in Russia largely through translations of works in Latin, German, Polish and Czech, and towards the end of the seventeenth century one or two tales were written which show some affinity with the Western European novels. The tale of *Savva Grudcyn*, though based primarily on a miracle story, has as its protagonist a young man who sells his soul for love of a woman and who subsequently undertakes a journey in company with the devil and goes through a series of adventures. He eventually repents and is redeemed at the intercession of the Virgin Mary. The tale of *Frol Skobeev* depicts sympathetically a rascally thief who, by seducing and abducting the daughter of a wealthy landowner, and enlisting the help of influential patrons to reconcile his new father-in-law to the match, contrives to make his own fortune. These tales, one of which deals

[1] Nikolai Gogol: *Dead Souls*, trans. and intro. by David Magarshack (Harmondsworth 1961), p. 11.

with the themes of temptation, sin and repentance within a framework similar to that of the picaresque novel, and the second of which deals with the success story of a strongly picaresque character, indicate that precedents did exist in Russian literature. The influence of the tradition could, however, have reached Gogol in a variety of ways and through a variety of sources, and it would be idle to speculate here about any one of them.

Such is the span of works dealt with in this volume. It has of course no pretensions to completeness, and its range has been determined chiefly by the interests of the people concerned. Since most readers will probably not be familiar with all the languages involved, bibliographies consist primarily of works in English. In spite of the circumscribed nature of the book, however, I hope that the general reader may find matter to interest him and that the specialist may be induced to make some comparisons which he might otherwise not have made.

C.J.W.

SOME GENERAL CRITICAL WORKS

ALTER, R. B.: *Rogue's Progress: Studies in the Picaresque Novel* (Cambridge, Mass. 1964).

BATAILLON, M.: *Le Roman picaresque* (Paris 1931).

CHANDLER, F. W.: *The Literature of Roguery* (Boston and New York 1907, republished Burt Franklin 1958).

— *Romances of Roguery; An Episode in the History of the Novel . . . Part I: The Picaresque Novel in Spain* (New York 1899, republished Burt Franklin 1961).

HEIDENREICH, HELMUT (ed.): *Pikarische Welt; Schriften zum europäischen Schelmenroman* (Darmstadt 1969).

MILLER, S.: *The Picaresque Novel* (Cleveland 1967).

PARKER, A. A.: *Literature and the Delinquent; The Picaresque Novel in Spain and Europe, 1599–1753* (Edinburgh 1967).

CHRISTINE J. WHITBOURN

Moral Ambiguity in the
Spanish Picaresque Tradition

P. E. RUSSELL HAS REFERRED TO 'THE AMBIGUITY INSEP-
arable from great works',[1] and while I am not sure that ambiguity is always a necessary concomitant of greatness, there can be
no doubt that many of the finest literary works do lend themselves
to a variety of interpretations. It is my intention to suggest in this
essay that an element of moral ambiguity has existed in the
Spanish picaresque tradition from earliest times and, continuing
throughout the Golden Age, constitutes one of its major points of
interest and its principal sources of strength.

One of the earliest precedents of the picaresque novel in Spain
is the *Libro de buen amor* or *Book of Good Love*, of Juan Ruiz, Archpriest of Hita, written between 1330 and 1343. This is an account
in autobiographical form of the love affairs of a priest and has many
of the characteristics of the picaresque novel as it eventually
developed, although it is written in verse, not prose. The tale
begins by the priest making one or two unsuccessful advances to
women, and there then follows a long debate with the god of love,
to whom the Archpriest complains of his lack of success. The god
advises the Archpriest about his choice of mistress and go-between,
and the Archpriest finds himself a go-between who thereafter
conducts his affairs for him with varying degrees of success.
Finally she dies, which effectively puts an end to his flirtations.
However, although the actual events of the story are frivolous
enough, they are interspersed by a series of discourses on such
subjects as death, the power of money, penitence, the world, the

[1] 'Ambiguity in *La Celestina*', *BHS* XL (1963) 35–40, at p. 36.

flesh and the devil, and the passion of Christ and, in spite of the irony and humour which characterize the autobiographical episodes, these discourses are presented quite seriously. The epitaph Juan Ruiz composes for his go-between, who belongs to the comic tale, may be ironic; the general reflections on death, which are an essential part of the didactic element, are not.

There are various respects in which this very heterogeneous but outstandingly lively work may be said to foreshadow the picaresque novel: (i) in its first-person technique; (ii) in the discreditable nature of the protagonist's activities; (iii) in the contemporary setting, in which real place-names are constantly identified and homely objects referred to; (iv) in its creation of an extremely lively procuress, whose type figures quite largely in subsequent picaresque novels; (v) in its constant use of irony and innuendo; (vi) in its moral ambiguity. The Archpriest makes various statements about his intentions, all of them deliberately ambiguous. In the prose prologue to the work, he writes:

> The law says: and they shall cast out and despise the evil arts of worldly love, which brings perdition on the soul and causes it to fall under the wrath of God, which shortens life, brings dishonour and ill fame, and grievously damages the body. But as to err is human, if there should be any who wish to indulge in a little lovemaking (and I do not advise it) they will find here some ways of going about it.[1]

Not only are his statements of intention ambiguous, but so is the work itself. Arguments in favour of love are presented with as much apparent conviction as those against it. The Archpriest's flirtations are conducted with a verve and enjoyment which communicates itself to the reader and encourages him to be a partisan. The liveliness of the amorous episodes makes them attractive, and this to some extent negatives the strictures of the moralist, and although serious topics are not for the most part flippantly treated, the passage from serious to comic is often so rapid as to be somewhat equivocal.[2]

---

[1] *Libro de buen amor*, ed. J. Corominas (Madrid 1967), pp. 77–79.
[2] For a discussion of the dualism of the *Libro de buen amor* see ' "Con miedo de la muerte la miel non es sabrosa": Love, Sin and Death in the *Libro de buen amor*', by Roger M. Walker in '*Libro de buen amor*' *Studies*, ed. G. B. Gybbon-Monypenny (London 1970).

Another work frequently referred to as an important antecedent of the picaresque novel is *Lo spill* or *The Mirror*, written in 1460 by Jaume Roig, a Valencian doctor. This is again a story told in the first person, and written in verse. In general conception it is a good deal closer to the picaresque novel as it ultimately developed than is the *Libro de buen amor*. First of all, more information is supplied about the protagonist's background, and his life story is very much more complete. Like many *pícaros*, he had a poor start in life. On the death of his father he is turned out of the house by his mother, and is therefore effectively an orphan. Thereafter the story deals with a series of picaresque adventures, in almost all of which the protagonist suffers at the hands of women. He marries three times, and all his wives turn out to be disastrous; on another occasion he narrowly escapes marriage, having discovered in time the deplorable character of his intended bride. The story continues up to a period which promises to be near the end of his life, when he finally attains peace by avoiding the company of women altogether. His attitude towards them is implacable. As with most anti-feminist works, it is difficult to determine how genuine is the desire to instruct, and to what extent the author was preoccupied with the denigration of woman either through malice or for his readers' entertainment. Roig insists throughout that his is a work of instruction, written for a nephew of his, but this was a not uncommon device, and need not necessarily imply a sincere moral aim. He does also suggest, like the Archpriest of Hita, that his work may be interpreted in various ways:

> If you are diligent and attend closely you may easily find sustenance to your satisfaction; feed upon whatever most appeals to you: flowers, fruit, leaves, roots or trunk, every reader will quickly find what he wants, according to his own taste and inclination; and be sure that you have read all before complaining.[1]

Unlike the Archpriest, however, who intersperses moral discourses among a few autobiographical episodes apparently selected at random, Roig's account of his hero's life is detailed, coherent, and largely uninterrupted. His narrative is continuous for the

---

[1] *Spill, o libre de les dones per mestre Jacme Roig*, ed. R. Chabás (Barcelona 1905), ll. 742–58.

first two parts of the work, and his philosophical reflections are contained chiefly in the third, and to a lesser extent in the fourth, part of the work. The lack of moralizing digressions makes the story fast-moving and very readable, but at the same time it makes one question whether instruction was really the author's primary object. The concentration of the didactic material in one area of the book undoubtedly improves its artistic quality, but it does not necessarily convince one of the sincerity of Roig's didactic aim. One is left with the same doubts about the morality of the work as with the *Libro de buen amor*. Roig does, however, introduce all the familiar picaresque background of street and inn and market, and many real place-names are mentioned. The technique is episodic, as the protagonist travels from place to place, recounting his various adventures. In Paris he stays at an inn where human flesh is served up in a pasty, an episode which foreshadows Pablos's visit to his uncle's house in Quevedo's *Buscón*.[1] Roig also describes a variety of scenes from contemporary life such as the women in the Valencian market,[2] the kind of punishment meted out for different sorts of crimes[3] and the holding of jousting competitions on New Year's Day.[4]

The adventures of Roig's protagonist normally involve encounters with the opposite sex, and the picture he paints of society is limited almost exclusively to women. His work is therefore much more limited in scope than subsequent picaresque novels, which depicted a far wider range of activities. At the same time Roig, like the picaresque writers, sees love as a deception and marriage as a snare, and his protagonist finally undergoes a religious conversion of questionable sincerity. R. Miquel y Planas has made it clear that there is little likelihood of Roig's work having exercised a strong and direct influence on the Castilian picaresque novel, because it was not generally known.[5] It does, however, show certain picaresque tendencies which no extant Castilian work of that period shows with the same clarity.

More directly influential than either the *Libro de buen amor* or *Lo spill* is Fernando de Rojas's *La Celestina* (1499), a dialogued novel

[1] Ibid., ll. 1647–1743.   [2] Ibid., ll. 7486–7537.
[3] Ibid., ll. 1759–62, 3336–55 and 1417–26.   [4] Ibid., ll. 1647–57.
[5] *El 'Espejo' de Jaime Roig, traducido al castellano y precedido de una introducción al 'Libro del Arcipreste de Talavera' y al 'Espejo' de J. Roig por R. Miquel y Planas* (Barcelona 1936–42), pp. CXIII–CXIV.

in twenty-one acts in which the central figure is a witch/procuress similar to Juan Ruiz's Trotaconventos, but whose character is developed in greater detail. In the story Calisto, a young nobleman, falls in love with Melibea, who is also of noble lineage and, being unable to approach her himself, employs Celestina at the instance of Sempronio, one of his servants. His other servant, Pármeno, endeavours to dissuade his master by painting Celestina in her true colours, but he is unsuccessful, and Celestina subsequently bribes him to hold his tongue by promising him the favours of Areúsa, a prostitute for whom he has a fondness. Celestina and the two servants agree to share the profits from the affair, but Celestina later tries to cheat them, and they murder her and are in their turn hanged. By Celestina's agency Calisto gains access to Melibea but his happiness is short-lived, as he falls from a ladder as he climbs back over her garden wall, and is killed. Melibea then commits suicide by throwing herself from the top of a tower. Celestina dominates the piece, though she is killed in the twelfth act; she arranges everything—satisfies the eager, persuades the reluctant— and what occurs after her death arises chiefly from action taken by her during her lifetime. She and the two servants and their prostitute mistresses are essentially picaresque types, and the situation of the servant who helps to forward his master's love affairs occurs later between Guzmán de Alfarache and the French ambassador. Pármeno in particular may be seen as a forerunner of the Golden Age *pícaro*. He has the disreputable background so common among later *pícaros*, and he has also the fundamental sense of justice and morality that one finds in Lazarillo de Tormes before he has come into contact with the world. The weaning of Pármeno from his loyal stand and the ultimate bringing about of his downfall is an essentially picaresque theme—the corruption of a young person by a deceitful world.

As with the works previously discussed, there arises once again the question of whether or not the author had a genuine moral aim in writing the work.[1] At the outset he specifically maintains that it is aimed at those young lovers who idolize their mistresses. All the principal characters except Celestina are tempted by love and give way to it; Celestina, though the eloquent advocate of love,

---

[1] For a fuller discussion of this question, see M. Bataillon: *'La Célestine' selon Fernando de Rojas* (Paris 1961) and P. E. Russell: 'Ambiguity in *La Celestina*'.

is in her old age ruled rather by avarice. All are punished for their sin or their credulity by death, so that there is a kind of poetic justice. At the same time, the author avoids judging any of them, or pointing out specifically the moral lesson which can be derived from the fate of each. It is also noticeable that in each case there are some extenuating circumstances which make the reader more sympathetic towards individual characters. One sees in detail the struggle which takes place between Melibea's inclination and her conscience; she does not give way easily. The corruption of the young and morally upright Pármeno is tragic. Calisto, a young man of twenty-three, has no wiser counsellor than a servant some years his junior. The prostitutes, on the other hand, display an unexpected loyalty and affection towards their lovers and protectors, and even Celestina herself, the most actively evil of all the characters, has an attractive liveliness and a strangely convincing belief in her own corrupt philosophy of life. These qualities or circumstances have the effect, if not of excusing error, at least of making it more understandable, and they make it difficult for the reader to regard any of the characters as wholly unsympathetic or wholly evil. One is therefore left with a feeling that the punishment was more severe than the sin merited, and that young love is attractive rather than otherwise.

Stylistically, *La Celestina* is closer to the picaresque novel than the other two works I have discussed. First of all, it is in prose, and secondly, it integrates the high and low styles to a greater extent. As might be expected, Calisto and Pleberio, the father of Melibea, express themselves in more rhetorical terms than the servants, and popular speech is chiefly put into the mouths of the low-life characters. Both Pármeno and Celestina, however, are capable of rhetoric, and Celestina in particular is inclined to change her style of speech to suit her interlocutor[1] or in accordance with the subject she is discussing. The separation of styles is still apparent, but the way was already paved for the *pícaro* to turn philosopher.

The majority of the Spanish picaresque novels were written during the first half of the seventeenth century, and were the

---

[1] The influence of the interlocutor on the style of speech of Celestina herself is discussed by María Rosa Lida de Malkiel in *La originalidad artística de 'La Celestina'* (Buenos Aires 1962), pp. 524–7, and was brought to my attention in connection with other characters by Professor A. D. Deyermond in a lecture given in the University of Hull on 6th March 1969.

product of what the critics have termed 'the age of disillusion-ment'. The optimism of the Renaissance had given way to a disenchantment with contemporary life, and the prevalent attitude was one which sought to expose abuses and dispel illusions, and which therefore made a bid not merely for realism, but for exag-geration of the ugly and the sordid. For me, the novels fall into two distinct categories. The first consists of those which continue the tradition, clearly established by the precedents I have discussed, of moral ambiguity. The protagonist in these novels is a delinquent or a ne'er-do-well who aspires to rise in the world by using his wits to cheat his fellows, and he is for the most part a social inadequate. The novels I propose to consider under this head are the anonymous *Lazarillo de Tormes* (1554), Mateo Alemán's *Guzmán de Alfarache* (1599–1604), Francisco de Quevedo's *La vida del buscón* (1626) and, though of inferior literary quality to the other three, the supposedly autobiographical *Estebanillo González* (1646). In the second group of novels, although the background is similar and the same sort of events occur, there is a strong consciousness of right and wrong. The protagonists are either not delinquent or only mildly or occasionally so, and they are not normally social inade-quates. In this category I include Vicente Espinel's *Marcos de Obregón* (1618) and three of Cervantes's *Novelas ejemplares: La ilustre fregona, Rinconete y Cortadillo* and *El coloquio de los perros* (all published together in 1613, although probably written at quite different times).

Since a gap of almost half a century separates the publication of *Lazarillo de Tormes* and its nearest successor, *Guzmán de Alfarache*, it is customary to regard *Lazarillo* as a precursor of the genre, and *Guzmán* as its first definitive example. However, as *Lazarillo* is very much more closely related to the seventeenth-century novels than are the precedents I have been discussing, I propose to consider it with the other novels. Lázaro's background, like most of the protagonists of the picaresque novels, is of the poorest. His father is convicted of swindling and, after being exiled, is killed in a battle against the Moors. His mother forms a liaison with a negro, who is later also convicted of stealing, though he thieves in order to provide the family with the necessaries of life. Eventually, a blind man offers to take Lázaro as his servant, and then Lázaro's inde-pendent life begins. The blind man teaches him all manner of cunning tricks, but does not give him enough to eat, so that he is obliged to resort to deception in order to survive. When he is discovered, the punishment is needlessly cruel, and this arouses the boy's resentment, and encourages him to take an equally cruel revenge on the blind man before he leaves him. His next master is a priest, who turns out to be even meaner than the blind man. For some time Lázaro contrives to keep alive by stealing bread from the chest in which the priest keeps the church offerings. His deception is, however, discovered and he is dismissed with the cruellest beating he has yet received. He then attaches himself to a promising-looking nobleman, thinking that here at least food will be plentiful, but he soon discovers that his master is as poor as himself, but is intent on maintaining appearances. The boy is reduced to begging to provide for both of them, and he does this until the rent for their house falls due, when his master simply disappears. Thereafter, Lázaro serves several masters, becoming more and more inured to deception and dishonesty, until he finally attains his ambition of getting an official post, when he becomes town crier of Toledo. He subsequently marries the mistress of an Archpriest, thus securing for himself a variety of modest material benefits, and resolutely refuses to listen to those solicitous neighbours who try to tell him that his wife is deceiving him. The prologue to this work once again hovers between an aim to instruct and an aim to entertain:

> I am of opinion, that things so worthy of memory, peraduenture neuer heard of before, ne seene, ought by all reason to come abroad to the sight of many & not be buried in the endlesse pit of obliuion, there perpetually to be forgotten: for it is possible that those, which shal reade this treatise of my life, may finde some pleasure therein. Wherfore true it is that *Plinie* recordeth, *there is no booke so euil, but hath some goodnesse in it contained* (considering all men tast not alike) that which one man will not eate, another longeth sore for: we see many despise things which other do greatly esteme: Therefore nothing ought to be broken and cast away vnles it were detestable, but that first diuers men should see the same, & especially being not hurtful, but rather able, in steade of damage, to yeeld profite & vtilitie.[1]

[1] *The Pleasaunt Historie of Lazarillo de Tormes a Spaniarde, wherein is conteined his marueilous deedes and life, With the straunge aduentures happened to him in the seruice of*

The story itself, too, leaves the reader in some doubt as to its moral intention. It is told in the first person and is recounted as if it were a success story, though the official post Lázaro finally attains is of the poorest. His apparently happy marriage is an illusion, but as time has gone on necessity and a corrupt society have so blunted his moral sensibilities that he will accept cuckoldry for the sake of the material benefits it brings with it. The privation he suffers early in life has taught him the value of these benefits, and his experiences with the nobleman have taught him to keep up appearances at all costs. Lázaro, however, bears comparatively little responsibility for his corruption; it starts with the example of his family, and continues with that of his masters, none of whom gives him any formal education or instils any moral principles in him. Lázaro is corrupted, but in the early stages of the book he shows innocence and kindness, and in the latter stages he is neither embittered nor tortured. His scope for choice is far more limited than that of Guzmán or Pablos, and his comparative contentment with his lot gives the work a more optimistic quality. Also his activities, unlike those of later *pícaros*, are hardly criminal. The only people from whom he steals are his first two masters and then only because of their extreme meanness and his own intense hunger. Thereafter, when he has no employment, he prefers begging to stealing. He connives at the imposture of the pardoner, but has no real part in it, and the life he has worked out for himself at the end of the book, although dishonourable, is not criminal. At the same time, he has none of the clear uprightness of Marcos de Obregón or of Carriazo and Avendaño in *La ilustre fregona*, and only rarely does he show that his actions are governed by other principles than that of expediency. In *Lazarillo de Tormes* there is therefore scope for two interpretations: it may be seen as a rather naïvely told tale in which the reader is invited to laugh at the protagonist's ingenuousness in regarding his own career as a success, or it may be regarded as a very subtle and sensitive account of the gradual corruption and ultimate degradation of a poor child by the world in which he lives.

Lazarillo, whether or not one regards it as a true picaresque

---

sundrie Masters. Drawen out of Spanish by Dauid Rouland of Anglesey (London 1586), fol. Aiii. The original Spanish can be found in *La novela picaresca española*, ed. A. Valbuena Prat (6th ed., Madrid 1968), p. 84, col. 1.

novel, certainly contains the germs of the picaresque tradition as it
eventually became established: the protagonist's disreputable
background; the episodic technique in which the protagonist
himself is the chief, though not the only, link; the degeneracy and
cruelty of contemporary society; the impostures of the low-life
types; love and marriage seen as a deception and betrayal; and
above all, the portrayal of a developing character corrupted by his
contact with the world. Not only are there similarities in the
material used, but various stylistic characteristics which are to be
found in *Lazarillo* also became very noticeable in subsequent
novels. For much of the work the tone is rather sententious, and
there is frequent mention of God: 'My father whome God pardon,
had the charge of a Mill . . .'[1] and again '. . . I came by helpe of
good people, to this noble citie of *Toledo*, where (I thanke God) my
wound closed up'.[2] Punning and euphemism also occur frequently,
though it is always made plain when a phrase is euphemistic; the
reader is clearly intended to see through what is, after all, merely a
verbal imposture.

Lazarillo de Tormes was followed, after a gap of nearly fifty years,
by *Guzmán de Alfarache*, the first part of which was published in
1599 and the second part in 1604. In this work a moralizing aim is
frequently apparent, and yet the same tradition of overall ambiguity
to which I have referred elsewhere is preserved in this novel too.
At the beginning of both parts, Alemán affirms the sincerity of his
moral intention. In the preamble addressed to the 'Discreet Reader'
he says:

> I know full well (considering the rudenesse of my wit, and
> shortnesse of my studies) that it had beene very fit in me to
> feare the Careere that I am to make; and that this libertie and
> licence of mine is more than needed, and might well have been
> spared; But considering with myselfe, that there is not any
> Booke so bad, out of which some good may not be drawne, it
> may be possible, that in that wherein my wit was wanting, the
> zeale which I had to profit others, may supply that defect, by
> working some vertuous effect; which happinesse if I light vpon,

---

[1] *The Pleasaunt Historie . . .*, fol. Av *recto*. *La novela picaresca española*, p. 85, col. 1.
[2] *The Pleasaunt Historie . . .*, Dvii *verso*. *La novela picaresca española*, p. 96, col. 2.

it shall bee a sufficient reward of my greater paines, and make this my boldnesse more worthy your pardon.[1]

In the first chapter of the second part Guzmán reaffirms his aim of instructing:

> My purpose only was (as I told thee before) to benefit thee, and to teach thee the way, how thou mightest with a great deale of content and safetie, passe thorow the gulph of that dangerous sea wherein thou saylest.[2]

These statements are unequivocal, and the substance of them is repeated several times over in the preambles to both parts. But even in the preface to the first part, Alemán suggests that the reader may have some licence in his interpretation of the work, and that it is certainly part of the author's aim to entertain him:

> In this Discourse, thou maist moralize things, as they shall bee offered vnto thee; Thou hast a large margent left thee to doe it; That, which thou shalt find lesse graue, or discomposed, presents it selfe in the person of a **Picaro**, or **Rogue**; which is the subiect of this Booke. Such things as these (which are not very many) sport thy selfe a while with them, iest & play the wagge, and afterwards shake hands with them. For at great Feasts, we must haue meats for all mouthes; and dishes for all tastes; Pleasant and sweet wines, which must cheere the heart, and helpe digestion; and musicke for to please and delight the eares.[3]

Here entertainment is clearly represented as subsidiary to moral improvement, but it is nevertheless admitted as a legitimate palliative of the moral lesson, and it is conceded that even the moral of the work is open to individual interpretation.

The work itself is somewhat similar in technique to the *Libro de buen amor*: comic episodes from Guzmán's life are interspersed with perfectly serious sermons on a wide variety of topics. The autobiography is far more detailed and complete, and the moralizing material wider-ranging, but the technique is similar. I am not of

---

[1] *The Rogue: or the Life of Guzman de Alfarache,* [trans. James Mabbe] (London 1622). *La novela picaresca española,* p. 236, col. 2.

[2] *The Rogue . . .,* p. 3. *La novela picaresca española,* p. 390, col. 2.

[3] *The Rogue . . .,* from the prologue addressed to the 'Discreet Reader'. *La novela picaresca española,* p. 237, col. 1.

course suggesting any direct influence, which would be unlikely, as the *Libro de buen amor* seems to have been very little read in the sixteenth and seventeenth centuries. One cannot but remark, however, how certain essential characteristics have persisted.

Guzmán has the poor background which one associates with the *pícaro*: his father was a rascally usurer and his mother a woman of doubtful virtue. He leaves home while still young, and meets with a variety of adventures in Spain and Italy, making a living for the most part by thieving and trickery. In the course of his life he has several opportunities to reform: the first occurs when an Italian cardinal takes him into his household out of charity; the second when Guzmán decides to pursue his studies for the priesthood at Alcalá; and the third when he is condemned to the galleys for life. The first two opportunities he ultimately rejects; the third he apparently accepts, and his life story is written in a supposed state of penitence.

Various considerations, however, militate against the reader's acceptance of Guzmán's conversion. The first is that his apparently conscientious exposure of a plot by a group of criminals to over-throw the normal forces of justice is also in his own best interests, as he is thereby able to curry favour with the authorities and secure his own freedom. The freedom is secured by a betrayal of his companions, which results in the death of two of them and the punishment of the rest. Guzmán may therefore be said to have recovered himself by an act of treachery, and an act of treachery, moreover, which could well have had its roots in a wholly unworthy desire for revenge. Guzmán's life has been governed principally by his own interest, and this final episode, carefully represented as having worked the miracle of his conversion, could in fact be regarded in the same light as any other, except that the reader is not given the opportunity to witness his subsequent backsliding when the moment of danger is past. The second consideration which renders Guzmán's conversion suspect is the fact of his having rejected opportunities to change his way of life in the past. He recognizes and admires the disinterested charity and humanity of the Italian cardinal, but he has not shown himself able to emulate it. He is capable of moments of true remorse, but the next time temp-tation comes in his way he yields to it; the reader may justifiably doubt his ability to make a sustained effort to live virtuously. On the other hand, although Guzmán has been portrayed as a youth lacking in stability and real strength of character he has consistently shown a strong preoccupation with spiritual things. He is lively and intelligent, and shows some conscience even in the picaresque episodes, so that the contradiction between his past behaviour and his sudden conversion is not absolute and it is possible to give credence to his conversion. It is, as J. A. Jones points out, a measure of Alemán's genius that he has contrived to reconcile with extraordinary skill and consistency two approaches to the problems of sin and delinquency and to leave his reader free to put his own interpretation upon the ultimate fate of his hero.

The same essential weakness as has already been noted in Guzmán is discernible also in the character of Pablos in Quevedo's *La vida del buscón,* although his aspirations are social even more than materialistic; he is primarily a status-seeker. His home background is of the lowest, his father being a thief who is eventually hanged, and his mother, with Quevedo's characteristic fondness for exaggeration, combining the offices of prostitute, procuress, lesbian and witch. By dint of serving a well-to-do young nobleman, Pablos contrives to get himself a university education and, having then left his master, he tries to advance himself in the world by means of a series of tricks and deceptions. He is, however, thwarted in every affair of any importance, and he sinks lower and lower, finally becoming involved in a murder in Seville, and escaping to the Indies as a fugitive from justice. Quevedo's technique is, however, quite different from Alemán's. Whereas Alemán's prefaces for the most part reveal a fairly clear didactic aim, Quevedo is deliberately ambiguous:

> You will find in this book all sorts of roguery (in which, I think, most people are interested), tricks, deceptions, inventions, and dodges, born of idleness, for living at the expense of others, and you will be able to gain much profit from it if you give heed to its warnings. And even though you should ignore the warnings, take note at least of the sermons, though I doubt whether anyone will buy a book of rogue's tricks to turn him away from the promptings of his natural depravity.[1]

[1] *The Life and Adventures of Don Pablos the Sharper, an Example for Vagabonds and a Mirror for Scamps,* trans. Francisco Villamiquel y Hardin (Leicester 1928), p. 9. *La novela picaresca española,* p. 1092, col. 1.

Unlike Alemán, Quevedo makes no attempt to moralize in the course of the history itself and when, at the end of the work, he hints that Pablos's downward course continued in the Indies and that his persistent ill fortune was due to his own mistaken way of life rather than to any other cause, the reader is at once struck by the lack of such comments elsewhere. It would be perfectly possible for anyone who had no thought of any underlying moral to take the work at its face value as a merely comic one, whereas it would be difficult to do so with Alemán's novel. Yet in spite of the lack of direct moralizing, the morality of Pablos's life story is clearer than Guzmán's. Pablos tries, by deception and trickery, to find a quick way to a position of dignity and respect and, because his methods are fundamentally wrong, he persistently fails. His gradual degeneration, and the various causes of it, are clearly and convincingly demonstrated. His course is consistent and realistic, and there is no question of any sudden conversion. The same kind of poetic justice is meted out as in *La Celestina*. But just as in *La Celestina* the harshness of the ultimate fate of the characters is mitigated by a sympathetic demonstration of their moral struggles, so the insight the reader has into Pablos's mind, and the knowledge of his disreputable background and his own shame at it, serve to excuse his wrongdoing to some extent. He is a weak character, in that he is offered the opportunity to lead an honourable life and refuses it in the hope of being able to rise more quickly by dishonourable means, but the effect on him of his family circumstances and early life is portrayed with such sensitivity that it is impossible not to regard him with sympathy. This circumstance, counteracted as it is by Quevedo's brilliant display of wit and almost complete avoidance of direct moralizing, fulfils the promise of ambiguity which is made in the prologue, blurring the distinction between right and wrong.

Estebanillo González (1646), the last of the novels I propose to consider in this group, differs from *Guzmán* and *El buscón* in one important respect: the identification of author and protagonist. Although the other two novels are written in the first person, there is no question of their being authentic autobiographies, and the author is able, at least in his prologue, to detach himself from his creation and state his own views. In *Estebanillo*, however, which professes to be a true autobiography and which may in fact be so, the prologue and the conclusion must be consistent with the character of the protagonist as it appears in the rest of the work. Unlike many Spanish *pícaros*, Estebanillo came from a background which, though poor, was honourable. His father made two attempts to have him taught a trade, but Estebanillo would have none of it and, having behaved badly in his apprenticeship, was dismissed by one master and ran away from the other. He subsists at first on a life of petty crime, and thereafter lives by currying favour with the great, becoming a jester in the households of the highest nobility, and maintaining his position by wit and flattery. He is a habitual and beastly drunkard and an abject coward, without dignity and without honour. His only interest in his family lies in the hope of an inheritance. His character is more or less static, his vices merely becoming accentuated as the tale wears on, but it is developed with a remarkable consistency. A. A. Parker has described *Estebanillo González* as 'a completely heartless book',[1] and so it is. In life and death, love and courage, in every generous impulse, Estebanillo finds matter for mirth and ridicule. Only his noble protectors escape his malice, and he loses no opportunity of including elaborate eulogies of them, and professions of the deepest respect and gratitude. It is therefore not surprising that he should maintain in his prose prologue that his book is intended for the delectation of these people:

> I am not publishing it for the sake of profit, but rather that it may serve as a gift and a solace for lords and princes and persons of rank, and I will not turn away my face or draw back my arm should they offer me any rewards; for where taking is concerned I am a man who will take a bribe, and as for accepting, I will accept any insult.[2]

He could hardly have summed up his own character more succinctly. Some of the laudatory verses at the beginning of the work refer to the valuable lessons of experience, and Estebanillo himself here and there gives a hint of a moral that could be drawn from his tale, but these few isolated comments count for nothing by the side of his constant facetiousness. However, the very degeneracy of Estebanillo produces a revulsion of feeling in the reader. One can

---

[1] In *Literature and the Delinquent* (Edinburgh 1967), p. 77.
[2] *La novela picaresca española*, p. 1721, col. 2.

excuse the errors of Lazarillo because of one's knowledge of his upbringing and his fundamental kindness, and one can sympathize with the mortification suffered by Guzmán and Pablos, both of whom have sympathetic qualities and many disadvantages to overcome. Estebanillo has neither the disadvantages nor the redeeming features. He is causelessly vicious and a wholly unsympathetic character and, as such, he arouses indignation and contempt in the reader. He attempts to invest his degraded life with a kind of spurious respectability and invites the reader to laugh at his various discreditable escapades. He resolutely refuses to see anything wrong in his way of life, but although he does not judge himself, the reader judges him, and so do other characters in the book, many of whom resent or despise him. Unquestionably, *Estebanillo González* has not the same subtlety in its development of character, nor the same complex relationship between fable and moral that one finds in the three great novels with which I have just compared it. Nevertheless it is not without artistry, and its morality may be greater than it has habitually been given credit for. If one considers the question of rewards, Estebanillo does not fare particularly well. He lives from hand to mouth throughout the novel and, because he is dependent upon the caprice of a great man, can hardly hope for any greater security in the future. Moreover, a court jester, although in some respects a privileged person, was not one of dignity or consideration. In his book Estebanillo is striving to justify himself, but he does not succeed in doing so, and although circumstances make it impossible for any serious moral intention to be asserted, right and wrong are here sufficiently interlinked and confused to allow one to affirm the same basic ambiguity, though not the same depth of insight, as in the other three novels.

It is precisely this moral ambiguity, stemming from the earliest precedents of the picaresque novel in Spanish literature, that is one of its most essential and persistent characteristics, and which may account in some measure for its considerable popularity. It was a formula which, at best, could combine realism, wit and instruction. The group of novels I have been discussing have in common a very strong realism, which does not attempt to portray the picaresque life as either admirable or attractive. They also have in common a protagonist who is socially inadequate and morally weak and who, although perhaps capable of distinguishing between right and wrong, is incapable of adhering steadily to a right course.

The second group of novels I wish to discuss are those in which the protagonist is either not a delinquent or only marginally so. In Vicente Espinel's *Marcos de Obregón* Marcos only has recourse to any criminal act in self-defence; it is either because he is wrongfully accused or deliberately attacked, and is therefore morally justified. He is honourable, wise, experienced and widely travelled, and it is emphasized that he is an old man looking back over his past life. Marcos's travels extend to Spain, Italy and Africa, and the variety of autobiographical episodes, as well as fables, anecdotes and discourses, is considerable. Marcos is highly civilized (he shows courtesy, poetic ability and musicianship) and essentially law-abiding. He is, however, resourceful enough to take effective measures to defend himself when placed in a difficult situation, and has enough liveliness of mind for his comments on others to have from time to time an entertaining streak of malice. In structure this novel resembles other picaresque novels, in that it treats of the travels and experiences of a character of modest social rank, and recounts a series of incidents in which the protagonist is the chief link. However, although the family background of Marcos is vague, it is certainly not depicted as disreputable, and the fact that he does not live by dishonourable or discreditable means has sometimes led critics to suggest that this is not a true picaresque novel. Espinel states clearly in his preface that his aim is both to entertain and to improve, and the rest of his work bears out his intention. Moral discourses are intercalated among the events of the tale, the protagonist's actions and philosophy of life are for the most part highly edifying, and where there is any departure from accepted standards, the circumstances render it quite unexceptionable. The distinction between right and wrong is very clear, and the protagonist steady in his pursuit of what is right. There is no ambiguity; virtue is extolled and vice and malice deprecated, and a way of life is demonstrated which, while it may not lead to a high degree of material prosperity, at least secures for the protagonist an honourable place in society and the respect of his fellow men. The existence of a genuine autobiographical element in this work (there are certain circumstances and incidents which coincide with events in Espinel's own life) may be at once a source of strength and one of weakness; it ensures the freshness and liveliness which come from actual experience, but has the effect also of detaching the *pícaro* somewhat from his surroundings. Marcos studies the society in which he lives and, more than any of the other *pícaros*, gives the impression of being an observer of the life he is describing.

Although there are many picaresque types depicted in *Don Quijote*, Cervantes's most important excursions into the realm of the picaresque are in the *Novelas ejemplares*, or cautionary tales, three of which have decided affinities with the tradition. These stories, however, like *Marcos de Obregón*, are distinguished by a very definite sense of right and wrong. In the tale of *La ilustre fregona*, the picaresque element is almost incidental to the main story, which is one of romantic love. The two protagonists, boys of noble background on their way from their native city of Burgos to study at Salamanca University, decide to abandon their studies and embrace the picaresque life. As they journey southwards, they call at an inn in Toledo, where one of the boys falls in love with a beautiful serving-wench. Thereafter the tale revolves round the wooing and winning of the serving-wench, who ultimately turns out to be of noble birth, and an eminently suitable wife for the young nobleman. While one *pícaro* is engaged in the pursuit of love, the other becomes involved in a series of picaresque adventures.

There are various features which separate this story from the novels I have placed in the first group. The first is its structure, which is quite compact, and not of the episodic kind one associates with the picaresque novel. The main plot is concerned with the love affair between Avendaño and Constanza, and the sub-plot with Carriazo and his picaresque associates. The second major difference is that the two *pícaros*, though they may act irresponsibly, do not act criminally. Apart from appropriating the funds provided by their families for their support at university, they never actually steal, or break the law in any way. They also show themselves virtuous, rejecting the improper advances of the ladies of easy virtue at the inn, and they show generosity and discretion. Love is depicted as a noble and romantic sentiment and marriage seen as the happy solution of the doubts and difficulties of courtship. In this tale two distinct worlds can be seen: that of the noble boys, with its clear responsibilities and rigid moral standards, which they carry with them; and the picaresque world, which has only a superficial attraction for them, and constitutes a romantic or decorative element in the tale rather than introducing a realistic or criminal element. The feature of it which is chiefly emphasized is its attractive freedom: freedom from responsibility, from the obligations of rank, from family ties. Ultimately, however, these responsibilities cannot be escaped, and the picaresque careers of the two boys end by a voluntary resumption of them in their proper background. The tale makes no attempt to present a realistic picture of low life, and the dénouement has all the improbability of a fairy tale. The treatment is lighthearted and ironical, and the inclusion of songs and dancing strengthens its ornamental character, and shifts emphasis away from those sequences which might have lent themselves to a realistic treatment.

The *Coloquio de los perros* is in some ways the most fantastic of all the tales, in that it purports to be a conversation between two dogs overheard in a poorhouse, when one of them recounts his life story to the other, and the two discuss it. Apart from the fable itself, however, the story is much like the life of a *pícaro*, treated this time in a highly realistic manner and in such a way as to constitute a serious attempt at social criticism. The technique is the familiar episodic one, and different categories of people are passed in review as the dog Berganza recounts his experiences with different masters. Deception and dishonesty are rife, but they are judged by the dogs, who apply the highest moral standards. Berganza often expresses surprise at the trickery he has witnessed, and if he fails to point a moral, his companion will draw his attention to it. The characters with whom Berganza has come into contact are almost without exception bad, and the tale reaches its climax in Berganza's encounter with a witch who represents an extreme of human evil, being in league with the devil. In spite of the generally low moral standards of the characters portrayed, however, the prevailing mood is not one of pessimism. The fantastic dogs maintain the standards that man is shown to have betrayed, and the reader is shown honour as well as dishonour. Moreover, there is no ambiguity. The distinction between right and wrong is made very clearly, not only in the behaviour of Berganza towards his various masters, but also in his and his companion's comments in retrospect. The moral rectitude and strength of character represented by the two dogs is not to be called in question.

It is otherwise with the third of these tales, *Rinconete y Cortadillo*, and for this reason I regard it as the most closely related of Cervantes's writings to the mainstream of Spanish picaresque tradition. The two boys are dirty, ragged, from poor homes, and they make their living by cheating and petty theft. They meet at an inn and journey together to Seville, where they begin to steal, but are told that if they are to continue to do so, they must join the thieves' fraternity, to which they are then introduced. The rest of the tale is devoted to painting a detailed picture of the members of this fraternity, and its grotesque chief, Monipodio. There is no formal plot, as there is in *La ilustre fregona;* the story resembles rather a chapter from a picaresque novel published in isolation. It has certain features that are highly realistic, such as the descriptions of the physical appearance of the boys themselves and of Monipodio, and the very detailed picture painted of the thieves' den and its equipment: the red brick patio, the bench with one leg missing, the broken pitcher and jug, the rush matting and the stoup for holy water. There is also an attempt to render the style of speech of the gang adequately by the extensive use of thieves' cant. Nevertheless the effect is not entirely realistic, and the picaresque world, and the two *pícaros* in particular, are still somewhat glamorized. The treatment of the whole gang and its activities is sufficiently burlesque as to render them comic rather than alarming. Monipodio behaves like a king giving audience, and the anti-climax of his appearance makes him ludicrous, not intimidating. This comic quality is further emphasized by the numerous malapropisms which are put into his mouth, and by the undignified way in which he scuttles for cover when danger threatens. These features all combine to reduce the realism of the tale and increase the impression of a world of illusion.

As regards the question of moral ambiguity, *Rinconete y Cortadillo* is closer to the tradition which links *Lazarillo, Guzmán* and *El buscón* than are Cervantes's other stories. The protagonists live by cheating, and no direct strictures are passed either on them or on cheating in general. F. W. Pierce has, however, pointed out that a definite distinction is drawn between the boys and the gang:[1] the boys are shown to be better educated, more courageous, more honourable and straightforward, and of stronger independent

[1] In 'Reality and Realism in the *Exemplary Novels*', BHS XXX (1953), 134–42.

judgment. They, like the reader, are amused at the antics of the gang, and therefore stand somewhat aloof from it, preserving their own integrity. At the end of the tale it is hinted that their association with the gang will not be a long one, and two different levels of moral degeneracy are clearly established. Even when the boys have made up their minds to stay with the gang, the decision is excused on the grounds of inexperience, and Rinconete in particular reveals a critical attitude which amounts to clear moral condemnation. Towards the end of the tale Rinconete's views are made known to the reader:

> He was no less astonish'd at the Obedience and Respect all of them paid *Monipodio*, being a clownish, cruel, and wicked Fellow; he consider'd what he had read in his Memorandum Book, and the barbarous Employment they all follow'd: Lastly, he exaggerated the Carelessness of the Magistrate of that famous City of *Seville*, for suffering such an inhuman and pernicious Set of People almost publickly, and he propos'd to advise his Companion, not to stay long in so wicked and dissolute a Company.[1]

The boys are not weak, but they are inexperienced and it is this lack of experience which is responsible for their taking the wrong course. Again, therefore, there arises a moral ambiguity which brings *Rinconete y Cortadillo* closer to the novels of the first group.

I have attempted to show that in the treatment of picaresque themes in Spain there has been from earliest times a moral ambiguity which became a central feature of the tradition, and which is very clearly discernible in the greatest of the sixteenth and seventeenth-century novels. This moral ambiguity is often bound up with the weakness of character of the protagonist and with his capacity for self-deception. These novels are strongly realistic, and depict the picaresque life as unstable and demoralizing. At the same time there existed a tradition with a stronger tendency to idealize the life of the vagabond, depicting it as romantic and attractive, and creating protagonists who were not necessarily criminal. Both categories may have a moral aim, in the first case

---

[1] *Two Humorous Novels, viz. A Diverting Dialogue between Scipio and Bergansa . . . and The Comical History of Rinconete and Cortadillo*, trans. Robert Goadby (London 1741), pp. 182–3. *La novela picaresca española*, p. 195, col. 2.

more often implicit and in the second, usually explicit. That both types enjoyed considerable popularity not only in Spain but also in the rest of Europe is testified by the number of editions, translations and imitations published all over Europe throughout the seventeenth and eighteenth centuries.

BIBLIOGRAPHY

Texts

CERVANTES SAAVEDRA, M. DE: *The Illustrious Chambermaid,* in *A Collection of Select Novels,* trans. Harry Bridges (Bristol 1728).
— *Three Exemplary Novels,* trans. S. Putnam (London 1953). (This includes both *Rinconete and Cortadillo* and *The Dogs' Colloquy.*)
— *Two Humorous Novels; A Diverting Dialogue between Scipio and Bergansa . . .* and *The Comical History of Rinconete and Cortadillo,* trans. Robert Goadby (London 1741).

GONZÁLEZ, ESTEBANILLO: *The Life of E. G., the pleasantest and most diverting of all comical scoundrels,* in *The Spanish Libertines,* trans. Captain John Stevens (London 1707).

QUEVEDO Y VILLEGAS, FRANCISCO DE: *The Life and Adventures of Buscón the Witty Spaniard. Put into English by a Person of Honour* (London 1657).
— *The Life and Adventures of Don Pablos the Sharper,* trans. Francisco Villamiquel y Hardin (Leicester 1928).

ROIG, JAUME: *Spill, o libre de les dones, per Mestre Jacme Roig,* ed. Roque Chabás (Barcelona 1905).
— *El 'Espejo' de Jaime Roig,* trans. and intro. R. Miquel y Planas (Barcelona 1936–42).

ROJAS, FERNANDO DE: *La Celestina,* ed. J. Cejador y Frauca (Madrid 1913).
— *The Spanish Bawd,* trans. James Mabbe (London 1631).
— *The Spanish Bawd,* trans. J. M. Cohen (Harmondsworth 1964).

RUIZ, JUAN, Archpriest of Hita: *Libro de buen amor,* ed. J. Corominas (Madrid 1967).
— *The Book of Good Love,* trans. Elisha K. Kane (New York 1933). Reissued, ed. J. E. Keller (Chapel Hill 1968).

TWO SPANISH PICARESQUE NOVELS: Lazarillo de Tormes; The Swindler, trans. Michael Alpert (Harmondsworth 1969).

VALBUENA PRAT, A. (ed.): *La novela picaresca española* (6th edn., Madrid 1968):
— ★Alemán, M.: *Guzmán de Alfarache*, pp. 233–577;
— Cervantes, M.: *El casamiento engañoso y Coloquio de los perros*, pp. 196–232; *La ilustre fregona*, pp. 150–76; *Rinconete y Cortadillo*, pp. 177–95;
— Espinel, V.: *La vida de Marcos de Obregón*, pp. 921–1087;
— González, Estebanillo: *Vida y hechos de Estebanillo González*, pp. 1719–1848;
— *Lazarillo de Tormes*, pp. 83–111;
— Quevedo, F. de: *La vida del buscón*, pp. 1089–1153.

Critical Works

CERVANTES SAAVEDRA, M. de:
Atkinson, W. C.: 'Cervantes, El Pinciano and the *Novelas ejemplares*', *HR* XVI (1948) 189–208.
Entwistle, W. J.: 'Cervantes, the Exemplary Novelist', *HR* IX (1941) 103–9.
Pierce, F. W.: 'Cervantes' Animal Fable', *Atlante* III (1955) 103–15.
Pierce, F. W.: 'Reality and Realism in the *Exemplary Novels*', *BHS* XXX (1953) 134–42.
Waley, Pamela: 'The Unity of the *Casamiento engañoso* and the *Coloquio de los perros*', *BHS* XXXIV (1957) 201–12.

ESPINEL, V.:
Haley, George: *Vicente Espinel and 'Marcos de Obregón'* (Providence, R.I. 1959).

LAZARILLO DE TORMES:
Jones, R. O.: Introduction to his edition of *La vida de Lazarillo de Tormes* (Manchester U.P. 1963).
Tarr, F. Courtney: 'Literary and Artistic Unity in the *Lazarillo de Tormes*', *PMLA* XLII (1927) 404–21.
Wardropper, B. W.: 'El trastorno de la moral en el *Lazarillo*', *NRFH* XV (1961) 441–7.
Willis, R. S.: 'Lazarillo and the Pardoner: The Artistic Necessity of the Fifth *Tractado*', *HR* XXVII (1959) 267–79.

QUEVEDO Y VILLEGAS, Francisco de:
Dunn, P. N.: 'El individuo y la sociedad en *La vida del buscón*', *BH* LII (1950) 375–96.
Lázaro Carreter, F.: 'Originalidad del *Buscón*', in *Studia Philolgica: Homenaje ofrecido a Dámaso Alonso* II (Madrid 1961), pp. 319–38.

★ For bibliography of this work please see pp. 46–7.

Morris, C. B.: 'The Unity and Structure of Quevedo's *Buscón: Desgracias encadenadas*' (University of Hull Occasional Papers in Modern Languages, No. 1, 1965).

Parker, A. A.: 'The Psychology of the pícaro in *El buscón*', *MLR* XLII (1947) 58–69.

ROJAS, Fernando de:

Bataillon, M.: '*La Célestine*' *selon Fernando de Rojas* (Paris 1961).

Gilman, S.: *The Art of 'La Celestina*' (Madison 1956).

Lida de Malkiel, María Rosa: *La originalidad artística de 'La Celestina*' (Buenos Aires 1962).

RUIZ, Juan, Archpriest of Hita:

Gybbon-Monypenny, G. B. (ed.): '*Libro de buen amor*' *Studies* (London 1970).

Lecoy, F.: *Recherches sur le 'Libro de buen amor' de Juan Ruiz* (Paris 1938).

Lida de Malkiel, María Rosa: *Two Spanish Masterpieces: The 'Book of Good Love' and the 'Celestina*' (Urbana 1962).

Zahareas, A. N.: *The Art of Juan Ruiz, Archpriest of Hita* (Madrid 1965).

J. A. JONES

The Duality and Complexity of *Guzmán de Alfarache:* Some Thoughts on the Structure and Interpretation of Alemán's Novel

P RAY, MASTER NED, HAVE YOU EVER HAD WIT ENOUGH to read a Spanish Novel called 'The Adventures of Gusman d'Alfarache'?—Not you, I'll be sworn;—and so, as nobody else reads it neither, and for the same reason because nobody knows what's worth reading, I shall refer them to the 'Rules, or Orders,' there laid down for the Government of the 'Hospital of Fools'.[1]

Guzmán de Alfarache was, indeed, a book worth reading, but fewer and fewer people seemed to think so around the year 1806 when James Beresford published *The Miseries of Human Life,* from which the above extract is taken. In fact, the initial success of Alemán's novel and its popularity in the seventeenth and eighteenth centuries are in marked contrast with the relative obscurity in which it was submerged for most of the nineteenth and early twentieth centuries. The general reader's lack of interest in

---

[1] Quoted by J. Fitzmaurice Kelly in introduction to *The Rogue or The Life of Guzmán de Alfarache,* trans. James Mabbe (*The Tudor Translations,* second series, ed. Charles Whibley, London and New York 1924, 4 vols.), Vol. I, p. ix. English quotations from *Guzmán de Alfarache* will be from this edition and Spanish references in footnotes will be to the Aguilar volume of *La novela picaresca española,* ed. Angel Valbuena Prat (6th edn., Madrid 1968).

Guzmán was matched, if not outshone, by the apathy of the literary specialist—Hispanist and non-Hispanist alike—who rarely ventured into the picaresque world of Guzmán or of any of the other Spanish *pícaros*.

The result of this neglect by both reader and scholar was that superficial and erroneous views were propagated and, for a long time, went unchallenged.[1] For example, after the publication of Chandler's *Romances of Roguery*[2] at the beginning of this century, it was generally accepted that the Spanish picaresque novel had very loose structure, if indeed it had any structure at all, and that it consisted of a superficial and cursory narration of episodes whose only connecting link was the rogue, or *pícaro*,[3] who moved from place to place and from master to master in an immoral and degenerate society. In his passage through this society, the *pícaro* became involved in humorous incidents which served to amuse the reader, especially by satisfying the latter's predilection for cruel realism and the scatological. The picaresque novel was thus essentially considered to be an episodic and light-hearted novel devoid of any structure or any moral and didactic purpose.

Fortunately, the last three decades have witnessed a revival of interest in it which has deepened our appreciation of the genre as a whole and produced balanced and profound studies of individual

---

[1] A. A. Parker, in *Literature and the Delinquent* (Edinburgh 1967), attempts to restore the balance, providing a penetrating and up-to-date study of the Spanish picaresque novel and its influence in Europe. Professor Parker's earlier study, 'The Psychology of the *Pícaro* in *El buscón*', *MLR* XLII (1947) 58–69, is indispensable.

[2] Frank W. Chandler: *Romances of Roguery: An Episode in the History of the Novel. In Two Parts. Part I, The Picaresque Novel in Spain* (New York 1899). See also *The Literature of Roguery* (London, Boston and New York 1907, 2 vols.) by the same author.

[3] Parker (*Literature and the Delinquent*, pp. 3–4) discussing the etymology of *pícaro*, makes the point that, in keeping with traditional and conventional views of the Spanish picaresque novel, this term has often been translated as 'rogue' but that nowadays a more apt rendering is 'delinquent', which denotes a dishonourable and anti-social individual who, in a mild way, offends against the moral and civil laws. This is what the seventeenth-century Spaniard understood by *pícaro*. Parker's use of 'delinquent' indicates the presence of a problem of personality and environment which raises complex moral and social issues. It was this problem that the best of Spanish picaresque writers explored. For further discussion on *pícaro*, see A. R. Nykl: 'Pícaro', *RHisp* LXXVII (1929) 172–86; T. E. May: 'Pícaro: A Suggestion', *RR* XLIII (1952) 27–33; O. F. Best: 'Para la etimología de pícaro', *NRFH* XVII, Nos. 3–4 (1963–4) 352–7; F. González-Ollé: 'Nuevos testimonios tempranos de pícaro y palabras afines', *Ib* I, No. 1 (1969) 56–8.

works.[1] In contrast with views such as Chandler's, the best of the Spanish picaresque novels have now been shown to be compact and closely-knit units, possessing a depth and wealth of meaning that elevate them to the rank of great works of literature. It can justifiably be claimed that the influence of Spanish literature at the beginning of the seventeenth century did not emanate only from Cervantes and *Don Quixote,* but also from Alemán's *Guzmán de Alfarache* and other important examples of the picaresque genre such as Quevedo's *Buscón.* It is the aim of this study to provide an analysis of Alemán's work that will illustrate its artistic merit, depth, and significance for the development of the novel.

Alemán's novel appeared in two parts. After the publication of Part I in 1599, a spurious second part appeared in 1602 which was the work of Mateo Luján de Saavedra, a pseudonym for a Valencian lawyer, Juan Martí. In the same way that Avellaneda's spurious continuation of *Don Quixote* hastened the publication of the true second part by Cervantes, Martí's work served as a spur to Alemán to publish the promised sequel to *Guzmán* in 1604. As with *Don Quixote, Guzmán* immediately became a best-seller, being translated into French, German and English, and earning vast fame and popularity for its author, whose qualities as a writer—later generously acknowledged by no less a figure than Baltasar Gracián[2] —were neatly summed up by Luis de Valdés in his 'Elogium to Mateo Alemán', preceding Part II of the novel:

If this be so; or if (as by evident Mathematical demonstrations) it shall require a necessary proofe of witnesses, let the best of the world be brought forth, I meane the famous University of Salamanca, where being celebrated there, by the best wits of that Academy, I have heard many speake of him, as the Grecians

---

[1] The following are especially helpful: F. C. Tarr: 'Literary and Artistic Unity in the *Lazarillo de Tormes*', *PMLA* XLII (1927) 404–21; P. N. Dunn: 'El individuo y la sociedad en *La vida del buscón*', *BH* LII (1950) 375–96; C. Guillén: 'La disposición temporal del *Lazarillo de Tormes*', *HR* XXV (1957) 264–79; R. S. Willis: 'Lazarillo and the Pardoner: The Artistic Necessity of the Fifth *Tractado*', *HR* XXVII (1959) 267–79; C. B. Morris: *The Unity and Structure of Quevedo's 'Buscón'* (University of Hull Occasional Papers in Modern Languages, No. 1, 1965).

[2] Baltasar Gracián y Morales (Belmonte 1601–Tarazona 1658); Spanish moralist and novelist and a Jesuit; author of *El héroe* (1637), *El político Fernando* (1640), *El discreto* (1646), *El oráculo manual y arte de prudencia* (1647); *Agudeza y arte de ingenio* (1648) and *El criticón* (1651–3–7).

of their Demosthenes, and the Romanes of their Cicero; reputing Mateo Alemán, as the Prince of eloquence in the Spanish tongue, as well for the modesty, and dextrousness of his style, as for his elegancies, and choice phrases. Of which opinion, was a religious Augustine, as discreet, as learned; who maintained in that University, in a publike Act, that there was not from the beginning of the world, to this present day, that the first Part of this was printed, any booke of like nature to this, (being no divine subject) of greater eyther profit or pleasure.

(Vol. III, pp. 10–11)[1]

Although Alemán's prose has, to a lesser or greater degree, continued to enjoy the praise of writers and critics, it is concerning the structure and interpretation of his novel that opinion has been sharply divided, and these two aspects will therefore be highlighted in this paper.

Firstly, let us examine the question of interpretation. *Guzmán de Alfarache* was an avowedly moral work, as Alemán himself tells us:

But considering with my selfe, that there is not any Booke so bad, out of which some good may not be drawne, it may be possible, that in that wherein my wit was wanting, the zeale which I had to profit others, may supply that defect, by working some vertuous effect; which happinesse if I light upon, it shall bee a sufficient reward of my greater paines, and make this my boldnesse more worthy your pardon.

(Vol. I, p. 16)[2]

This intention is re-stated several times in the opening sections of Part I and is reiterated at the beginning of Part II, where Alemán affirms that the object of his novel is 'to serve as a sentinell, to discover all sorts of Vices, and to draw treacle out of divers poysons:...' (Vol. III, p. 5).[3]

Alemán's preoccupation with the moral intent of his work requires some comment. In the first place, it has been suggested that it may have been the result of his Jewish ancestry. As a *converso*, a new Christian, he would be anxious to establish his

---

[1] Pt. II—'Elogios', p. 387. [2] Pt. I—'Del mismo al discreto lector', p. 236.
[3] Pt. II—'Al lector', p. 385.

orthodoxy.[1] In the second place, *Guzmán de Alfarache* has to be placed against a background of religious development which had repercussions in every sphere of Spanish life. Between 1546 and 1563, the Council of Trent debated and promulgated decrees that not only provided a Catholic response to the Protestant reformers but also called for reform and renewal at every level of Catholic life, not least in the intellectual and literary fields.[2] For example, the Tridentine decree on Scripture, setting up the Vulgate as the most authoritative biblical text, sparked off fiery debates in the universities. The fierce controversies over the Vulgate version at Salamanca University exemplified the clash between, on the one hand, the powerful traditionalist forces, represented by men such as León de Castro and Bartolomé de Medina,[3] and, on the other, the more liberal and balanced scholars such as Luis de León, Gaspar de Grajal and Martínez de Cantalapiedra.[4] The opposing currents of thought and outlook, perhaps best illustrated in the field of biblical criticism, were characteristic of every aspect of intellectual life and accounted for the tension and pressure experienced by writers and thinkers in Counter-reformation Spain.

In the literary field, the Council of Trent accentuated the didactic function of literature, which should be truthful and responsible.[5] Spanish writers of the Golden Age were constantly preoccupied by this matter.[6] Criticism of the novels of chivalry centred more on the way the novels affected their readers than on artistic considerations. This concern with the instructive and edifying aim of literature was especially evident in the sphere of poetry where many defences written on behalf of the Muses towards the end of

---

[1] R. O. Jones, in *A Literary History of Spain. The Golden Age: Prose and Poetry* (London 1971) p. 127, questions the whole *converso* background of Alemán, refusing to take it into account until new and more convincing evidence appears.
[2] For a discussion of the debates and decrees of Trent, see Hubert Jedin: *A History of the Council of Trent*, trans. Ernest Graf (London, etc. 1957–61, 2 vols.).
[3] Professors at Salamanca, bitterly opposed to the liberal approach to learning and scholarship exemplified by Luis de León and his followers.
[4] Branded as the judaizers of Salamanca because of the importance that they attached to the Hebrew text of the Bible in biblical exegesis. See the following works edited by Miguel de la Pinta Llorente: *Proceso inquisitorial contra el maestro Gaspar de Grajal* (Madrid 1935); *Proceso criminal contra el hebraísta salmantino Martín Martínez de Cantalapiedra* (Madrid 1946); *Estudios y polémicas sobre Fray Luis de León* (Madrid 1956).
[5] See Parker: *Literature and the Delinquent*, pp. 20–25.
[6] See E. C. Riley: *Cervantes' Theory of the Novel* (Oxford 1962).

the sixteenth century highlight the concern with the didactic purpose. For example, Pedro de Valencia, who in 1613 provided the first piece of Góngora criticism, had earlier felt impelled to write prefaces for two books of poems by his friend and mentor, Arias Montano, justifying and defending the use of poetry by the latter.[1] Luis de León's reticence concerning his own poems was also the result of the same tension. However, despite the concern with the didactic purpose of literature, the pleasure-giving aspects were gradually gaining prominence.

Alemán's work claimed to fulfil the twofold purpose of literature enunciated by Horace—to instruct and to entertain—as Alonso de Barros, chamberlain to Philip III, points out in his 'Elogium' to Part I:

> He hath formed this booke for us, mixing it with that most sweet harmony of delight and profit, which Horace requireth; inviting us with its pleasure, and instructing us with its gravity, taking for its scope, the publick good, and for its reward, the common benefit.
>
> (Vol. I, p. 24)[2]

It is a revealing fact that, although Alemán entitled the second part of his novel *Watch-Tower of Man's Life*, the work nevertheless became known as *Pícaro*. In other words, the lighter, entertaining aspects appealed more to the seventeenth-century public. Yet, Alemán's novel could still claim to answer to the Counter-reformation demands of truthfulness and responsibility, although, as we shall later see, there is room for argument as to the specific ways in which these conditions could be satisfied.

Recent studies of *Guzmán* have tended to affirm its clear didactic purpose and have presented the work as fulfilling certain religious aims. But there has been a division of opinion too, and the advocates of *Guzmán* as a novel of religious thesis have been opposed by those critics who see no religious significance in the work, or who consider the religious aspects as subordinate to social and peda-gogical questions, and by those who hold that the novel is anti-religious, or, at least, anti-Catholic. Among these latter critics one

---

[1] These works were *Poemata in Quatuor Tomos Distincta* (Antwerp 1589) and *Hymni et Saecula* (Antwerp 1593).
[2] Pt. I—'Elogio de Alonso de Barros', p. 238.

can cite G. Sobejano and J. A. van Praag, whilst E. Moreno Báez and, more recently, A. A. Parker, have argued forcibly and lucidly in favour of the religious interpretation.[1] Critics have followed one or other of these lines of approach, and few have assumed middle positions, although the possibility for wider and even differing interpretations of Alemán's work has been underlined by Otis H. Green, Donald McGrady and Celina S. de Cortazar.[2] However, these writers have not substantiated their claims by showing how the importance of the apparently clear-cut religious thesis can be diminished by the wider implications of *Guzmán de Alfarache*, or how the climactic impact of the conversion can, as a logical necessity, be questioned. This is what will be attempted in the pages that follow.

It is futile to adopt extremist and exclusive positions concerning the interpretation of *Guzmán de Alfarache*. Alemán's novel, like *Don Quixote*, is a long, complex, and suggestive book which can say something new with each reading of it.[3] The alacrity and determination with which conflicting interpretations have been defended

[1] Gonzalo Sobejano: 'De la intención y valor del *Guzmán de Alfarache*', RF LXXI (1959) 267–311; J. A. van Praag: 'Sobre el sentido del *Guzmán de Alfarache*', in *Estudios dedicados a Menéndez Pidal* (Madrid 1954), Vol. V, pp. 283–306; E. Moreno Báez: *Lección y sentido del 'Guzmán de Alfarache'* (RFE Anejo XL, Madrid 1948); A. A. Parker: *Literature and the Delinquent*, pp. 31–45.

[2] Otis H. Green: *Spain and the Western Tradition: The Castilian Mind in Literature from El Cid to Calderón* (Madison, Wis., 1963–6, 4 vols.) Vol. IV, pp. 217–18, 226–32; Donald McGrady: *Mateo Alemán* (New York 1968); Celina S. de Cortazar: 'Notas para el estudio de la estructura del *Guzmán de Alfarache*', Fi VIII (1962) 79–95.

[3] But there have been few fundamental studies of *Guzmán de Alfarache*, closer attention having been given to peripheral questions of biography, background, and sources. For a comprehensive bibliography, see Germán Bleiberg: 'Mateo Alemán y los galeotes', RO XIII (2ª época, 1966) 330–63, and E. Cros: *Protée et le gueux: recherches sur les origines et la nature du récit picaresque dans 'Guzmán de Alfarache'* (Paris 1967). After completing my own study, the following works have appeared: Francisco Rico: *La novela picaresca y el punto de vista* (Barcelona 1970); Alberto del Monte: *Itinerario de la novela picaresca española* (Barcelona 1971), which is a new and revised Spanish edition of the Italian original published in 1957; Angel San Miguel: *Sentido y estructura del 'Guzmán de Alfarache' de Mateo Alemán* (Madrid 1971); R. W. Truman has contributed a small section on Alemán in *The Continental Renaissance, 1500–1600*, ed. A. J. Krailsheimer (The Pelican Guides to European Literature, Harmondsworth 1971), pp. 336–40, and there is another section on *Guzmán* in R. O. Jones's *The Golden Age: Prose and Poetry*, pp. 125–32. It is reassuring to note that, in their different ways, these studies emphasize both the complexity of Alemán's novel and the wide variety of possible interpretations.

is illustrative of the mixed reactions it can provoke and should serve to warn that a balanced interpretation is to be found not at one of the extremes but somewhere in the middle, taking account of, and leaving the way open for, the many ideas which the novel seems to suggest. *Guzmán de Alfarache* is capable of more than one closed, tidy interpretation. It seems to me that one's reading of the novel can be enriched and its significance better grasped if its capacity to be interpreted in more ways than one is acknowledged. Many interpretations so far advanced have been either so exclusive as to misrepresent the work, or else so wide as to make it appear confusing and aimless. However, it is possible to widen one's perspective but yet to focus on definite guidelines which will lead towards a balanced understanding of the novel. For this purpose, it will be helpful to outline the plot briefly.

Guzmán is born in Seville, the illegitimate son of low and disreputable parents. His father is a usurer and his mother a dedicated prostitute. When his father dies, Guzmán decides to venture forth by himself in the hope of improving his position. After experiencing the difficulties of fending for himself and awakening to the corruption of the society that surrounds him, he joins a company of soldiers and goes to Italy intending to contact noble relatives. During his travels in Spain and Italy, Guzmán undertakes varied types of work; he is a stableboy at an inn, he serves as a cook, he becomes the attendant of an army captain, and later, of a cardinal who takes pity on him, and he is also engaged in service with the French ambassador in Rome. In between these periods of service, Guzmán joins the ranks of the *pícaros* in Madrid, and afterwards, the confraternity of beggars in Rome. From these two schools, he acquires the subtle tricks of a trade which he succeeds in mastering. His conduct throughout is characterized by deceit, fraud, theft, and gambling. In Italy, Guzmán is rejected by his relatives, an act for which he later has his revenge. He manages to amass considerable wealth through thieving and cheating at cards and eventually returns to Madrid as a wealthy and dishonourable merchant. He marries the daughter of a money-lender and she ruins him. On her death, the impoverished Guzmán decides to become a priest and goes to Alcalá, spurred on more by his desire to seek a comfortable and easy livelihood than by any deep and genuine sense of calling. The weakness of his determination is revealed when he falls passionately in love, abandons all idea of ordination and remarries. His wife, not an honourable lady, provides, through her prostitution, the easy livelihood that he is seeking. She eventually runs away with a galley captain and the abandoned Guzmán once again takes to the road of theft and gambling. He is finally caught by the authorities and sentenced to the galleys for life. It is there, in the depths of degradation and misery, that Guzmán at last answers the divine call which he has rejected at various points throughout his life, and he repents. The book ends with his conversion and the promise of a third part which never appeared.

The action is interrupted by a series of digressions, which we shall discuss later, and by four short stories, which we shall briefly examine at this point.[1] The four novelettes are divided equally between the two parts of the novel and can, in fact, be read separately although, as Donald McGrady has shown, they can be considered to form an integral part of the work. The common theme of the stories is love and they all have a moral aim, based on the underlying dual purpose of instruction and entertainment. Alemán obtained his material for these short stories from the Greek and Moorish novel, from courtly literature, and from the Italian *novella*.

The stories of Part I are entitled *Ozmín y Daraja* and *Dorido y Clorinia*. The former is a Moorish story which depicts chaste love and its reward in a happy Christian marriage; the latter contrasts with it. *Dorido y Clorinia* sets before us the tragic ending of two passionate lovers who do not pay heed to religious precept. The source of this story is medieval courtly literature. The two short stories thus complement each other. Virtue is rewarded in the first, whilst the disregard of it is punished in the second.

In Part II, this pattern is reversed. *Don Luis de Castro y don Rodrigo de Narvaez* portrays the punishment of licentious behaviour, whilst *Bonifacio y Dorotea* sets before us an example to be emulated. Both stories are based on the Italian *novella*.

The world of these four novelettes is a clear-cut one of right and

[1] See the following studies by Donald McGrady: 'Masuccio and Alemán: Italian Renaissance and Spanish Baroque', *CL* XVIII (1966) 203–10; 'Dorido y Clorinia: An Italianate *Novella* by Mateo Alemán', *RoN* VIII (1966) 91–5; 'Heliodorus' Influence on Mateo Alemán', *HR* XXXIV (1966) 49–53. See also G. A. Alfaro: 'El cuento intercalado en la novela picaresca', *HispI* XL, No. 1 (1970) 1–8.

wrong, good and evil, love and hate, reward and punishment. We witness situations which, by their clarity and unambiguous nature, contrast sharply with the rest of Alemán's work. Guzmán's world is thus thrown into relief. At the same time, the reader is offered an opportunity to rest and, in this way, the interpolated stories contribute towards the pleasure-giving aims of the novel as a whole.

In general, *Guzmán* possesses many of the basic characteristics of *Lazarillo de Tormes*.[1] Like the latter work, Alemán's novel is the autobiography of the *pícaro*, hence we have the double time sequence, namely, the moment of writing and the time of the action described, which affords the writer a means of putting the past into perspective. Guzmán, like Lázaro, also has a shady and sordid family background, the difference being one of degree only. Guzmán heaps sin upon sin on his parents; his father is a swindler, a thief and renegade, and a homosexual who is also irresistibly attracted by women. Guzmán's mother is an adulteress and a prostitute who is surpassed at her trade only by her own mother, for the latter is unable to tell her daughter with any degree of certainty who her father was. As in *Lazarillo*, the narrative is characterized by scatological and realistic details and by cruel humour. For example, when Guzmán is serving with the cook, he accidentally collides with his master's naked wife who, in her shock, has a sudden and uncontrollable movement of the bowels. At another point, we witness the rare sight in literature of a cardinal making use of his chamber pot. Many similar examples could be quoted.

If in these and other ways *Lazarillo* and *Guzmán* are similar, there are also many important differences between the two works. *Guzmán* is a far longer and more complex novel. It is difficult to read not only because of its length but also because of its complicated structure. The narration of Guzmán's experiences is constantly interrupted by a series of moral digressions that are difficult to reconcile with the person of Guzmán and with the events and actions that he describes. These digressions can be broadly divided into two categories: firstly, short, sententious statements and brief moralizing paragraphs, and secondly, long reflective and homiletic passages. The former are liberally interspersed through-

[1] For a detailed comparison between *Lazarillo* and *Guzmán*, see the article by Sobejano already cited.

out the narrative whilst the latter appear at certain points, sometimes forming a prelude to the experiences of Guzmán, other times
following sordid events described with a delectation that contrasts
with the moralizing tone. Alemán, fully aware of the blatant
conflict between, on the one hand, the protagonist's life and, on the
other, his thoughts and moral sensibilities, tried to forestall the
inevitable criticism with the following warning:

> And looke not thou on him that sayes it, but to that which is
> said unto thee.
>
> (Vol. I, p. 83)[1]

Although to some readers the structure of *Guzmán* will always
constitute an artistic weakness, it can be contended that this very
dualistic structure gives the work greater depth and significance.
In the same way that Don Quixote and Sancho Panza acquire
complete meaning only in relation to each other, so, in *Guzmán*,
the narrative events and the moralizing passages have to be
accepted jointly.[2] However, the question of structure is essentially
bound up with the general purpose of the work, and it is to this
latter point that we shall now devote our attention.

Perhaps the most forceful and widely-accepted interpretation of
Guzmán de Alfarache so far advanced is that first propounded by
Moreno Báez, who sees the work primarily as a novel of religious
thesis and considers it as an attempt to promote the Catholic
doctrine of temptation, sin, and repentance, which embraces
Original Sin, free will, the saving grace of God, and man's co-
operation with it. *Guzmán* is seen as an instrument of the Counter-
reformation, fulfilling the demands of truthfulness and responsibility.

The events of Guzmán's life appear to corroborate Báez's
theory. We see Guzmán struggling with temptation, falling into
evil ways, having the opportunity of repenting and reforming but

---

[1] Pt. I, Bk. I, Ch. II, p. 251.

[2] Richard Ellman, in *James Joyce* (London 1966), pp. 665–6, quotes the following
comments of Joyce on the expurgated parts of *Ulysses* which Alemán might well
have made with reference to his digressions: 'The whole point about them is that
they cannot be omitted. Either they are put in gratuitously without reference to
my general purpose; or they are an integral part of my book. If they are mere
interpolations, my book is inartistic, and if they are strictly in their place, they
cannot be left out.'

refusing, falling deeper and deeper into sin and misery, and eventually, in the abyss of moral and physical degradation, answering God's call, and starting out on a new life of spiritual and moral integrity. The work is therefore considered to end on an exultant note of spiritual salvation and moral regeneration.

It is not my aim to disprove the above theory, for the theological points alluded to can be clearly traced in the novel. However, it can be suggested that *Guzmán de Alfarache* has a relevance wider than the strictly religious, and that the spiritual message is not necessarily an optimistic one; the conversion of Guzmán need not constitute the joyous and hopeful climax that it is thought to be.

In order to grasp the full significance of the work, the religious question has to be viewed in conjunction with the social and psychological problems that the book poses. In this respect, two studies are worthy of mention, firstly, that of Sobejano, who opposes the religious thesis by presenting an equally convincing theory based on the pedagogical aims of the work, and secondly, Eoff's analysis of Guzmán, which underlines certain traits of character that are relevant to my own study.[1]

Sobejano discounts the religious interpretation which, he claims, derives from looking at the work with hindsight and not from the viewpoint of the original purpose. According to this critic, Alemán's aim is to show how a reckless young man, devoid of moral guidance and at the mercy of his passions, falls into degradation, being goaded by a degenerate and immoral society. Sobejano emphasizes two main aspects of the pedagogical character of the work: firstly, the attempt to teach by portraying what must be rejected, and secondly, criticism of different social types and situations in an effort to show how society should function for the common good. It is from this twofold pedagogical aim, Sobejano claims, that the dualistic structure of the novel stems, and this structure is not one of opposition between the ascetic and the picaresque, between sin and divine grace, novel and sermon, but simply one that demonstrates the degeneration of a single individual and of society in general. This requires both narration of the evils to be avoided and reflection on the ways of reform. The account of Guzmán's life entertains whilst the reflections edify.

[1] S. Eoff: 'The Picaresque Psychology of Guzmán de Alfarache', *HR XXI* (1953) 107–19.

Sobejano's thesis is convincing but suffers from its limited and exclusive nature. It gives too little weight to the religious aspects and does not fully relate the narrative events to the moral digressions, which often dwell on religious matters which Sobejano dismisses. It is therefore possible to agree, to some extent, with his views, but it must be stressed that his interpretation, on its own, does not provide a balanced view of *Guzmán de Alfarache*. For our particular purpose, Sobejano's thesis serves to illustrate that the religious interpretation can be counterbalanced, and indeed, complemented by a radically different viewpoint.

Eoff's study illuminates Guzmán's character and analyses his development in contact with society. The significant stages of this development are three: firstly, Guzmán's initial confrontation with a cruel society, which leads him into the picaresque life, secondly, the life of an adolescent *pícaro*, and thirdly, the life of an adult *pícaro*. Underlying this transition from boyhood to manhood, from an innocent child to a consummate *pícaro*, a constant, determining psychological factor can be detected, namely, a desire to be in an approved social position, which leads Guzmán to seek the favour of those in authority or those who promise some form of reward. Eoff's study can be questioned on a number of points, but it is valuable in stressing the basic tendency in Guzmán's character to conform and to accept the path of least resistance, which is relevant to the final conversion.

The viewpoints so far examined taken together provide a sound basis from which to consider the novel. Varying interpretations emphasize different questions which, if taken together and not to the exclusion of each other, can reveal a measure of cynicism, scepticism and ambiguity that may otherwise pass by unperceived.

It can be argued that Alemán's novel does not only constitute an attempt to put forward specific religious or social teaching but is also concerned with emphasizing in a general way the value of, and the need for, individual and social responsibility. Through Guzmán and his contact with society, we are shown the relevance of truthful and responsible behaviour both for the individual and for society in general.

The work can be described as the analysis of the process of degeneration of a particular individual in a corrupt society, in the context of a specific religious theme of temptation, sin and repentance. In this way, *Guzmán de Alfarache* fulfils the Counter-reformation demands of truthfulness and responsibility. Alemán is truthful and responsible because he gives a realistic portrayal of an individual's experiences in society and tries to draw some helpful conclusions from this study. But the conclusions have up to now been somewhat over-stressed and misrepresented. Let us first examine how the religious thesis can be questioned, firstly, on its own merits, and secondly, in conjunction with the wider problems of personality and social relations raised by the novel.

If *Guzmán de Alfarache* puts forward Tridentine teaching on Original Sin, grace and free will, and if the conversion is the logical outcome of the methodical exposition of the process of temptation, sin and repentance, then it offers a message of hope and optimism. But these feelings are not necessarily the most easily or obviously provoked by our reading of the work. In fact, despite the conversion, we can be submerged in a marked mood of pessimism at the end of the novel. This paradox can be explained.

The pessimism of *Guzmán* derives from the consciousness of Original Sin and from the profound awareness of the equality of all men in sin that the work embodies, and which is briefly expressed by Guzmán as follows:

> Behold (brother) and see the Enterlude of our life is ended; our disguizes laid aside; and thou art as I; I, as thou; and all of us as one another.   (Vol. II, p. 114)[1]

Added to this preoccupation with man's lot in relation to sin is the repeated acknowledgement of the inherent weakness of human nature, the conflict of life on earth, and the mutability of earthly goods:

> Mans life is a warre-fare upon earth, there is no certainty therein; no settled assurance, no estate that is permanent; no pleasure that is perfect; no content that is true; but all is counterfeit and vaine.   (Vol. I, p. 147)[2]

Despondency and fatalism produce a stoical cynicism as an antidote to the disillusionment and frustration arising from the tribulations

---

[1] Pt. I, Bk. II, Ch. X, p. 334.   [2] Pt. I, Bk. I, Ch. VII, p. 269.

and struggles of life. Guzmán's moral and spiritual weakness is the sour fruit of this basic scepticism.

The pessimistic consciousness of sin is intimately connected with what in theological terms is known as the *fomes peccati*, the spark of sin, or that which inclines man towards evil, in other words concupiscence.[1] Towards the end of the sixteenth century, controversy centred on the exact meaning and implications of the *fomes*. Luther claimed that the *fomes peccati* in itself constituted sin, a view that denied the spiritual rebirth of baptism and took away from Christians the possibility of overcoming concupiscence and leading a life of grace. On the other hand, Tridentine teaching on this subject was based on St. Paul, who admitted the permanence of concupiscence which, he said, could be described as sin in a wide sense because it inclined man towards evil and made it difficult for him to follow God. In so far as concupiscence stemmed from and led to sin, it was part of sin, but man could struggle with it, co-operating in the work of justification, and meriting salvation.

Guzmán de Alfarache seems to waver between the Lutheran and Pauline positions. To some extent, the pessimism engendered by the work is counterbalanced by an almost equally vivid awareness of man's capacity to be saved through the exercise of free will, but the force of concupiscence is overwhelmingly felt:

> I cannot say, that my malignant Starre was the cause thereof, but that mine owne evill inclination was the worker of my woe; For the starres *non compellunt, sed inclinant*, they incline, but not constraine. They make men apt, but they doe not coact. Some ignorant fooles sticke not to say; O Sir, Destinie is not to be avoyded. That which shall be, shall be. And it is vaine to strive against it. I tell thee (my friend) it is a vaine thing to say so; and

---

[1] The effects of concupiscence are best illustrated by Guzmán's comments on Original Sin: 'From hence, grew that blindnesse in his understanding, that forgetfulnesse in his memory, that defect in his will, that disorder in his appetite, that depravednesse in his Actions, that deceit in his senses, that weaknesse in his strength, and those paines and torments, in his greatest delights, and pleasures. A cruell squadron of sore and fierce enemies; who, as soone as God hath infused our soules into our bodies, incompassing us on every side, violently set upon us; and so hotly assaile us with the sweet enticements of sin, faire promises, and the false apparances of foule and filthy pleasures, that they over-throw all goodnesse in us, and so taint and corrupt our soules, that they put them quite out of that good course, for which they were created' (Vol. IV, p. 223; Pt. II, Bk. III, Ch. V, p. 540).

thou doest not understand the truth thereof aright; for there is no necessitie, that it is, or should be so; it is thou thy selfe, that mak'st it so to be.

In these Morall and outward things, thou hast a kinde of free-will conferred upon thee, whereby thou maist (if thou wilt) governe both thy selfe, and thy actions. Thy starre cannot constraine thee, nor all the heavens joyned together with all the force and power that they have, cannot compell thee against thy will.

It is thou that forcest thy selfe to leave what is good, and to apply thy selfe to that which is evill, following thy dishonest desires, whence these thy crosses and calamities come upon thee.

(Vol. II, pp. 261–2)[1]

Guzmán is seen to live out the struggle with the *fomes*. He constantly struggles with and very often succumbs to temptation, as he himself confesses: 'I had often resolved to be good, but I was quickly weary of well-doing'; . . . (Vol. IV, p. 184).[2] The spark of sin burns brightly within him. But he can recognize his own weakness and give some semblance of the determination and resolution required to mend his ways. For example, Guzmán leaves the ambassador 'purposing with my selfe to make hereafter a new Booke, washing away by my vertues, those spots, which Vice had stained me with all' (Vol. III, p. 152).[3] Eventually, he is converted from his life of sin and degeneracy.

The nature of the conversion must be understood. It does not mean that Guzmán will in future lead a saintly life. His conversion consists of a realization and awareness of past failure and a determination to offer a fight in the future. In other words, it is only at that point that he decides to come to terms with concupiscence instead of being the willing victim of its motions. Alemán reveals his skill and artistry in the way that he portrays Guzmán's change of heart and yet develops his character logically. There is no sudden or dramatic change. Guzmán's actions in the future will, to a lesser or greater degree, be consistent with his past, but his strength to overcome temptation and sin and his chances of eventual salvation

---

[1] Pt. I, Bk. III, Ch. X, pp. 373–4.   [2] Pt. II, Bk. III, Ch. IV, p. 529.
[3] Pt. II, Bk. I, Ch. VII, p. 425.

have both been increased.[1] The conversion then is not so much a glorious affirmation of spiritual victory as a pointer to that which is required in order to set out on the road to the eternal life that, as Guzmán states in the closing lines of the novel, we all hope to attain. The work can thus be seen to end on a less triumphant but more realistic note.

Considering now the basic traits of Guzmán's character already underlined and his general attitude to society, there are even less grounds for optimism. Guzmán's actions throughout the novel are governed by self-interest and self-preservation. His behaviour is motivated by a desire for reward and social advancement, and in a difficult situation his cowardly nature leads him to take the easiest path out. Hypocrisy and pretence are the natural results of his lack of courage and conviction, as he himself confesses:

> And how often (having a bloudy heart, and a damnable intention, being naturally cowardly, timorous, and feeble) did I pardon, and put up injuries, putting them in publike to Gods account, mine owne thoughts secretly condemning me, did I in secret dissemble them, not sticking to say in publike, God be thanked for it; when as I was truly inwardly offended, and that no other thing in the world did hinder my revenge, but that I was fearefull, and found my selfe unable to put it in execution? But the coales thereof were alive, and did burne within my soule, whose flames I had much adoe to suppresse.
>
> (Vol. IV, pp. 284–5)[2]

It is difficult not to bear Guzmán's words in mind when we view the circumstances of his conversion. Guzmán has been condemned to the galleys for life. He feels weighed down by physical suffering and can see no remedy for his situation except by currying favour with his captors:

---

[1] Witness Guzmán's own words: 'Presently upon this, I treated of the frequent Confession of my sinnes, and of the reformation of my life, and of the cleansing of my conscience; in which good deliberation, I continued many dayes; but I was flesh and bloud. I did still stumble, almost at every step, and now and then tooke a fall. But for any proceeding in my accustomed evill actions, I was much amended, and went from that time forward reforming my former course of life' (Vol. IV, p. 329; Pt. II, Bk. III, Ch. VIII, p. 570).

[2] Pt. II, Bk. III, Ch. VII, p. 557.

Now, in the meane while, forasmuch as I did consider with my selfe, that wheresoever a man lives, hee had need of an Angell of guard to attend him upon all occasions; I beganne to bethinke my selfe whom I should make choyse of to bee my Protector. And after that I had thorowly thought there-upon, I could not finde out any fitter for my turne, then the Masters-Mate.

. . . .

Thus by little and little, I went scruing my selfe into his service, getting more ground still upon him, and striving to out-strip the rest: As well in my attendance at his boord, as in having him to bed; I trickt up his Cabin, brusht his Cloathes, kept them neat and handsome, lookt to his linnen, and was in every other respect so diligent about him, that within a few dayes I was the onely man in his eye. (Vol. IV, p. 318)[1]

It is in this situation, in the depths of despair and degradation, that Guzmán decides to mend his ways. His conversion may well be a final realization of his evil ways after having approached the edge of an abyss of nothingness. But we cannot help feeling that Guzmán is also being moved by his instinct for self-preservation. His change of heart is stimulated by the most basic and selfish motive of fear, and, although this may furnish a fully acceptable theological starting-point for the life of grace, it can equally fill us with doubt concerning Guzmán's sincerity, especially as he has already at another point in his life been prepared to prostitute the religious life for physical comfort and material sufficiency. Guzmán undergoes the conversion under pressure. Reform offers the only path out and he accepts it. His change of heart and soul can thus appear to be no more than another piece of opportunistic conformism in order to secure selfish ends. The conversion can be regarded in a more cynical and sceptical light, and the novel can be seen to end on a more ambiguous note than has hitherto been conceded. If we grant this measure of ambiguity, then we are perhaps half-way towards explaining the dualistic structure which has provoked so much criticism and debate.

It can be argued that the dual structure of the work is essential to its purpose. A basic duality has been underlined by C. Blanco Aguinaga, who draws attention to pairs of opposites such as good

[1] Pt. II, Bk. III, Ch. VIII, p. 567.

and evil, truth and falsehood, freedom and compulsion, all of which are necessary for the *desengaño*[1] theme of the novel, for Alemán attempts to show the right path by immersing the reader in the dirt and sin of the world, which he is bound to reject.[2] By presenting two sides of a question, Alemán can portray the reality and truth of matters and indicate the path of virtue and goodness.

The dualities indicated by Aguinaga can be detected both in the style, in which we can trace a carefully worked out balance of correspondences and oppositions, and in the structure, which is divided between the narrative events and the moral digressions. The narrative-digressive structure sets before us two sides between which there lies a wide gap: 'How farre, in this simplicitie of ours, are our deeds, from our thoughts!' (Vol. I, p. 239)[3] Alemán underlines the two extremes, 'deeds' (narrative) and 'thoughts' (digressions). The relation between these two extremes is crucial for, although the two sides presented are in apparent opposition to each other, they are nevertheless intimately connected. In the first place, the experiences of Guzmán's life, which should repel us, are recounted with evident gusto, whilst the reflections, which should instruct us, come from Guzmán himself, whose example we should shun. In this lies the paradox that has hindered a proper appreciation of the novel.

Critics have been unable to reconcile the narrative events with the digressions. On the one hand, attempts have been made to cut out the reflective passages, whilst, on the other, it has been affirmed that the digressions constitute the main substance of the work, the narrative events being only of secondary importance. Both of these viewpoints are erroneous. Unless one is prepared to accuse Alemán of a gross lack of artistry, the two aspects of the novel must be accepted jointly.

In fact, the significance of the dual structure can be appreciated by relating it to the ambiguity mentioned in relation to the

[1] *Desengaño* = 'disillusion'. Much of Golden Age literature in Spain attempted to portray things as they really are, thus dispelling the reader's illusions and bringing him face to face with truth and reality.
[2] C. Blanco Aguinaga: 'Cervantes y la picaresca. Notas sobre dos tipos de realismo', *NRFH* XI (1957) 313–42. An abridged English version of this article, entitled 'Cervantes and the Picaresque Mode: Notes on Two Kinds of Realism', can be found in *Cervantes: A Collection of Critical Essays*. ed. Lowry Nelson Jr. (New Jersey 1969), pp. 137–51.
[3] Pt. I, Bk. II, Ch. I, p. 297.

conversion. The structure of *Guzmán* increases the ambiguity by revealing a *sic et non* attitude. Alemán portrays two sides of a question and leaves the reader to make a choice which necessarily has to be based on the complementary views furnished by both narrative and digressions, for the digressions are skilfully placed by Alemán in order to produce the effect he wants. There are short sententious phrases liberally scattered throughout the novel, constantly reminding us of the opposition between good and evil, wisdom and the lack of it, and so on. There are also long reflective passages placed at certain points in the narrative providing opportunity for thought and meditation in the midst of the momentous and formative experiences of Guzmán's life. The connection between the events and the reflections is crucial. In some cases, the two taken together reinforce a moral point, in other cases they neutralize it, but yet in others the combination of light-hearted adventures and escapades with serious moral reflections tends to uncover a certain measure of cynicism stemming from the frustration and disillusionment of trying to reconcile the ideal and the real, reason and passion, truth and falsehood, good and evil. There is thus a two-way current; the moral reflections lessen the laughter provoked by Guzmán's experiences, whilst the latter weaken the force of the moral lesson. A balance is set up between action and reflection, laughter and seriousness, evil and virtue. Alemán's artistry lies in establishing and maintaining this precarious equilibrium throughout the work. The author sustains a relationship with the reader, who can tilt the balance in either direction by deciding how much of the cynicism and scepticism to accept and how much moral direction to reject. It is this ground for decision and interpretation afforded the reader that constitutes one of the most appealing features of the novel.

If one accepts what has been affirmed above about the conversion of Guzmán and the relevance of the dual structure to its ambiguity, how can the avowed didactic purpose of the novel be explained?

It must be stressed that the didactic aim of *Guzmán* does not consist solely of the propagation of certain Catholic dogmas nor of the criticism of particular social types and attitudes, nor of the portrayal of the sad fate that awaits the reckless impulses of youth, though all these points can be extracted from the text. There is a wider significance.

For a proper understanding of the novel it is important that we bear in mind the autobiographical form of the work. As in *Lazarillo*, the events narrated have to be constantly related to the mature narrator. The double time sequence thus introduced offers the writer a way of putting past events into perspective and of securing approval or condemnation of them from the reader. Alemán thus has a means of commenting on the whole situation. To some extent, he can identify with the boy Guzmán, to another extent he can sympathize with the mature narrator, and he can manipulate the relationship between the two to indicate his own personal feelings. Both the autobiographical form and the dualistic structure are vital instruments of self-expression for the writer.

Guzmán thus has to be considered not merely as the confession of Guzmán's life but as the reflection of Alemán's mind and soul. Alemán tries to portray the conflicts encountered in the world he lives in, and this assumes the double plane of man in general (Original Sin, *fomes*, etc.) and the problems of a particular individual in a particular society (Guzmán and his experiences), and all this as an expression of the tensions and conflicts felt within himself.

Alemán speaks to us equally through the narrative events and the moral digressions. He manoeuvres both towards a given end; there is a constant wavering between a light, carefree, perhaps cynical and sceptical attitude and a more serious, responsible and optimistic one, but both are felt with equal vigour. In his attitude to what he presents, Alemán meets the demands of responsibility, for he is genuinely concerned with the right behaviour of man. To the extent that he portrays this realistically and convincingly, Alemán meets the demands of truthfulness.

Indeed, the novel has to be seen under the spotlight of truth which is Alemán's prime concern and which embraces all the aspects mentioned. Alemán is concerned with emphasizing the necessity of truth as the basis of the individual's personality and of his relationships in every sphere of society. It is in this that the exemplariness of the work lies. Honesty, self-knowledge, truthfulness, all these are qualities which affect the whole personality and all human commitments. The need for this basic integrity is observed in Guzmán's life.[1] His weakness throughout the novel

[1] 'I say, that I was wholly compacted of lyes, as I had ever beene. With some I would be a Martyr, with other some a Confessor. For all things are not com-

derives from his inherent inability to come to terms with himself; he suffers from a basic self-deception which destroys any attempt at self-discipline and reform and which leads him to rationalize his own weak will and lack of determination.

Guzmán's basic falseness has to be seen in relation to society, which suffers from the same malady; deceit, corruption, immorality and selfishness engulf Guzmán everywhere.[1] The interplay between Guzmán and this society furnishes the essential picaresque theme and offers a means of analysing the problems of delinquency, against the more general and wider problem of man's struggle with sin and evil. Alemán focuses these problems from both a positive and a negative angle, hence the work is a mixture of optimism and pessimism, hope and despair, humour and seriousness, faith and scepticism, and the balance can be tilted in one direction or the other according to the sensibilities of each particular reader.

Guzmán de Alfarache is thus a moral work not so much because it puts forward specific doctrines or shows us the virtues of a particular way of life, but because it attempts to draw attention to basic conflicts and tensions of human life, and tries to establish the need for individuals and for society in general to confront these problems by constant adherence to truthful and responsible behaviour.

BIBLIOGRAPHY

Texts

ALEMÁN MATEO: *Guzmán de Alfarache*, in *La novela picaresca española*, ed. A. Valbuena Prat (6th edn., Madrid 1968), pp. 233–577.
— *The Rogue; or The Life of Guzmán de Alfarache*, trans. James Mabbe (London 1622, 2 vols.). A later edition of this translation was published in

municated to all. And therefore I would never truly impart my troubles to any, nor punctually publish them; but when I was forced to manifest the same, I would tell one man one tale, and another, another; and no man had it without its comment.' (Vol. III, p. 144; Pt. II, Bk. I, Ch. VII, p. 423.)

[1] 'Amongst so many friends, as I had, and did daily converse withall, I found very few, who had not an eye to the north-starre of their own proper interest, and shap't their course by the Compasse of their own private ends; having only a desire to deceive, not having any respect at all to the friendship they profest, being devoide of all love, truth, and shame: I was of an easie and tractable nature, my condition was facile and apt to be mis-led, their tongue was all honie, but their heart was very gall it selfe: whose bitternesse, I had too often tasted to my cost.' (Vol. III, p. 184; Pt. II, Bk. II, Ch. I, p. 434.)

The Tudor Translations, second series, ed. Charles Whibley (London and New York 1924).

Critical Works

ALEMÁN, Mateo:

Alvarez, G.: *Mateo Alemán* (Buenos Aires 1953).

Cros, E.: *Protée et le gueux; recherches sur les origines et la nature du récit picaresque dans 'Guzmán de Alfarache'* (Paris 1967).

Eoff, S.: 'The Picaresque Psychology of Guzmán de Alfarache', *HR* XXI (1953) 107–19.

McGrady, Donald: *Mateo Alemán* (New York 1968).

Moreno Báez, E.: *Lección y sentido del 'Guzmán de Alfarache'*, (*RFE* Anejo XL, Madrid 1948).

Oakley, R. J.: 'The Problematic Unity of *Guzmán de Alfarache*', in *Hispanic Studies in Honour of Joseph Manson,* ed. D. M. Atkinson and A. H. Clarke (Oxford 1972), pp. 185–206.

Praag, J. A. van: 'Sobre el sentido del *Guzmán de Alfarache*', in *Estudios dedicados a Menéndez Pidal* V (1954), pp. 283–306.

Ricapito, J. V.: 'Love and Marriage in *Guzmán de Alfarache;* an Essay on Literary and Artistic Unity', *KRQ* XV (1968) 123–35.

Sobejano, G.: 'De la intención y valor del *Guzmán de Alfarache*', *RF* LXXI (1959) 267–311.

J. M. RITCHIE

Grimmelshausen's *Simplicissimus* and *The Runagate Courage*

ONE THING THAT MUST BE REALIZED FROM THE START is that in discussing *Simplicius Simplicissimus* and *Courasche* one is not simply talking about two small novels. The titles, given here only in very abbreviated form, refer in fact to two figures from what have been called collectively Grimmelshausen's Simplician writings. He wrote a great deal besides in a great variety of different styles, but the Simplician works were the *Abentheurliche Simplicissimus Teutsch* in five books first published in 1668; to this was added a Continuation as Book VI; his publisher exploited the success of *Simplicissimus* with a book called *Viridarium historicum* which Grimmelshausen had not written at all, and about the same time a *Barock-Simplicissimus* came out with various additions, illustrations and stylistic alterations, plus three further *Continuationen*. Added to this there came a series of works *Courasche*, *Gaukeltasche*, *Springinsfeld*, *Ewigwährender Kalender*, *Ratstübel Plutonis*, *Vogelnest*, *Bartkrieg*, etc., from which emerge the four Simplician short novels *Courasche*, *Springinsfeld*, *Vogelnest I and II*. These were intended not only as deliberate counterparts to *Simplicissimus*, the author himself declared that he saw them as complementary parts of the cohesive whole. In his 'preface to the well-disposed reader' at the beginning of *Vogelnest II* he explains that *Courasche* was intended as Book VII of the *Simplicissimus* cycle, *Springinsfeld* as Book VIII and *Vogelnest I and II* as Books IX and X.

Hence the author himself thought of the *Simplicissimus* saga as complete in ten books. Clearly all this has a bearing on the reader, who is constantly aware that the author, by his various additions and expansions, is creating his own private cosmos. However, no matter how the works are read, the contrasting figures of Simplicissimus and Courasche are what really gives these rambling writings focus. Simplicissimus, of course, is there from the start, while the lady Courasche does not appear until Book V Chapter 6 of *Simplicissimus Teutsch:*

> At that time there resided in Sauerbrunnen a lovely lady who gave herself out to be of noble birth but was as far as I could see more *mobilis* than *nobilis*. On this same man-trap I paid court . . .

So 'La donna è mobile' is the characteristic mark of Courasche from the very first mention of her by Simplicius. In the *Courasche* novel things are viewed not from the male but the female point of view, for the lady herself assumes the rôle of narrator and gives her story in her own words. This is the only time this happens in the cycle of Simplician writings. When she reappears, for example in Chapters 4–6 of *Springinsfeld*, she is no longer the protagonist but only an incidental figure once again. From this it becomes apparent that one is dealing with an apparently rambling, sprawling, baroque mass of material—something like a seventeenth-century television serial, in which certain characters occasionally rise to prominence, for a time appear to assume a life of their own, and also to a certain extent decide the direction of the narrative, only to fade away once more into the background to make way for someone else.

To say that the characters assume a life of their own (not necessarily, however, one independent of the author) immediately marks out the most striking single feature of the Simplician writings. This quality of life is exactly what is lacking in most of the German literature of the seventeenth century. The *Simplicissimus* and *Courasche* novels are so full of life that they represent something of a miracle, a miracle that has puzzled and delighted critics and literary historians for over two centuries. For who can explain a miracle? What is 'life' in a work of literature? What makes one novel live while hundreds die? And where does the miracle come from? As the German works are being discussed in connection with the whole question of the picaresque tradition one answer to this last question must be at least in part—from Spain! But the Spanish *pícaro* cannot have been the only source of new blood for German literature. Other authors before Grimmelshausen had looked to Spain and failed to create living works. Nor did the contemporary German audience devour the tales of Simplicissimus because they seemed Spanish. Indeed their author was at pains, as the title *Simplicissimus teutsch* indicates, to stress the *German* qualities of his work, however much it may have its life-giving roots in foreign soil. However, devour the tales the German reader did, making them among the most popular ever.

If popularity in the sense of being close to the people, and responding to its tastes and needs is a quality of the picaresque narrative then the Simplician writings had this in abundance, as is evidenced by the reception they received right from the start and continue to enjoy to this day. Indeed the Simplician tales have proved popular in all senses of the word—they are what the Germans would call *volkstümlich*, meaning of the people and for the people. While so much seventeenth-century German literature seemed almost exclusively learned and aristocratic, this was work which seemed to offer an almost conscious contrast. Learned works tend to be rather dull. On the other hand by the nature of things Simplicissimus, at least in the beginning, is so far from being learned that he knows absolutely nothing, he is agreeably ignorant. This may be among other things one of the great German novels of education,[1] but if so it starts absolutely from scratch with a hero who is a complete *tabula rasa*. He does later in the course of his life spend a great deal of time with strange and curious books, but the educational process with which the narrative is concerned lays far more stress on the protagonist's experience in the world than is customary in German novels. One of the morals imparted by this didactic tale is that given to Simplicissimus by the hermit at an early stage in his education, namely *nosce te ipsum*, but this is demonstrated as much by the hero's outward path into real life as by his path inwards into contemplation and quasi-mystical self-awareness. Fortunately the other piece of advice which the young Simplicissimus is given, namely to avoid bad company, is ignored in practice—both Simplicius and Courasche spend more of their lives in bad company than in good and the narrative is all the livelier in terms of incident and excitement as a result. The temptations of the world are shown in all their glorious attractions

[1] Melitta Gerhard: 'Grimmelshausens Simplicissimus als Entwicklungsroman,' in *Der Simplicissimusdichter und sein Werk* (Darmstadt 1969), pp. 133–60.

and while the moral is constantly stressed in all cases, nevertheless vice has on the whole a rather better run for its money than virtue.

Simplicissimus is not only *teutsch* he is also *abentheurlich* and this too provides a clue to another source of all the life and vigour, for the form of the narrative proves in effect to be a string of war-time adventures. The locale may change constantly but the general setting remains the same, namely a world at war. All the Simplician writings are concerned with war and this is undoubtedly an important factor in the *élan* of the narrative. Tales of war and adventure have always been a fruitful source of popular entertainment and edification. However, Grimmelshausen is by no means a naïve story-teller who simply piles one gory incident on top of another. On the contrary his tales, which rely a great deal for their impact on their apparent spontaneity and factuality, turn out to be a long way removed from mere *reportage*. The historical reality of the Thirty Years' War is always there as a framework for all the extraordinary events in the lives narrated, but Grimmelshausen did not attempt to draw a picture of things as they really happened. *Simplicissimus* was written over twenty years after the end of all hostilities when the major peace treaties had long since been signed. So the feeling of immediacy, spontaneity and life which his narrative imparts is only apparent. In fact he does not record scenes from the heat of battle as they were unfolding, he never gives a mere chronicle of real events. Instead Grimmelshausen produces a work of reflection in which the first-person narrator looks back over a long life, assessing the significance of various incidents, commenting on a particular turn of events, and generally speaking revealing from the series of apparently unrelated trivia the major constituent themes in an age of upheaval and change. By the nature of things it is arguable whether the picaresque hero can be said to have any individual character, for the widely disparate incidents in which he plays the central rôle tend to militate against consistency of psychological development. Hence the protagonists Simplicissimus and Courasche are both shown to be significant not merely as lively individuals but as figures representative of the age in which they live and have their being. Grimmelshausen has cleverly turned the exciting picaresque narrative of war and adventure into a baroque epic of reflection and self-knowledge.

Nevertheless powerful and horrific events form the main ingre-
dients of the surface narrative, so much so indeed that Grimmelshausen's Simplician writings can be described collectively as a
'horror story' in which Catholics slaughter Protestants and
Protestants slaughter Catholics, all in the cause of religion. In this
he was by no means unique, for horror was a feature of the age as
the dramas of Gryphius and Lohenstein amply demonstrate. Yet
here again Grimmelshausen seems to stand out among writers of
his time by the way in which he combines true-to-life realism in
the depiction of the horrific with larger-than-life scale. Somehow
Grimmelshausen successfully registers both the sordid detail of
life in his time and the cosmic scope of it all. Hence his apparently
simple narrative grows until, for example, the passage of the simple
lad through the world becomes a kind of revelation whereby the
personal experiences of the narrator expose man's dilemma at the
depths into which the German-speaking lands had been plunged
by this long and deadening war. Cosmic references are of course a
common feature of baroque works, and even the most casual
reader cannot fail to notice pointers to Mars and Venus and the
various signs of the Zodiac throughout the work of Grimmelshausen, the author among other things of an 'eternal calendar'.
However, only the most recent and most intensive examination of
the baroque novel *Simplicissimus* has proved beyond any shadow of a
doubt that the whole structure of the cycle is fundamentally
astrological.[1] Günther Weydt has passed beyond accepted traditional descriptions of *Simplicissimus* as a mere adventure or horror
story to reveal the rôle which the planets have to play in it. In this
way the author consciously removes his heroes from the purely
private sphere and deliberately places them against a vastly wider
framework of cosmic forces.

Awareness of this complex structure somehow makes this
otherwise old-style novel very 'modern' and in view of all this it is
not surprising that twentieth-century readers have felt even more
closely akin to Grimmelshausen's Simplician writings than readers
in the eighteenth and nineteenth centuries. And it is not surprising
that a dramatist like Brecht should turn to the Simplician writings
for the main protagonist in his epic drama on the theme of war,

[1] Günther Weydt: 'Planetensymbolik im barocken Roman' in *Nachahmung und
Schöpfung im Barock: Studien um Grimmelshausen* (Bern 1968), pp. 243-300.

war not as an heroic exception but as a normal way of life, war which goes on and on. Nor was Brecht alone in turning to Grimmelshausen (and hence indirectly to Spain) to conjure up the nature of evil in the modern world. Around the same time Hofmannsthal too was reading Grimmelshausen's *Simplicissimus* and in the twenty-fourth and final chapter of the fifth book he found the lengthy extract from Guevara which shows 'why and how Simplicissimus left the world again'. This was exactly the section which he adopted for incorporation into his festival drama *Der Turm*. In addition the whole of the external action of *Der Turm* was based on Calderón's *La vida es sueño*, of which he had at one time written a free adaptation. Hofmannsthal's play is in fact a hybrid which borrows from many sources but the most significant borrowing was from Grimmelshausen's *Simplicissimus* in which he found the prototype for his Olivier, a corporal and new officer of the guard at the tower. Brian Coghlan sums up the significance of the Olivier figure as follows:

A peculiarly and fatefully contemporary figure. He is that kind of a rabble-rouser, a mixture of forceful and even magnetic personality, who has become so familiar in the mass totalitarian movements of the twentieth century.[1]

By the very mention of the name Olivier Hofmannsthal consciously brings into his play the analogy of the chaos of the Thirty Years' War. Olivier, at least as far as Grimmelshausen's novel was concerned, was the evil counterpart of Simplicius' good companion Herzbruder and in many respects the only truly picaresque figure in the whole cycle of Simplician writings, being exclusively a low-life character. Like so many other figures in the narrative the facts of this evil marauder's life are given with incredible realism of detail yet these facts serve only to create something larger than life, the very personification of evil. And just as Brecht found he could use the Courasche figure to give a twentieth-century audience a sense of the vastness of modern warfare, so Hofmannsthal exploited the potential of Olivier in the twentieth century as a portent of the Hitler-type dictatorship that was about to engulf the German-speaking lands so soon. What readers like Hofmannsthal and Brecht were doing was to single out the marked visionary and

[1] Brian Coghlan: *Hofmannsthal's Festival Dramas* (Cambridge U.P. 1964), p. 200.

prophetic quality of Grimmelshausen's narrative and stress parallels thus revealed between the seventeenth and the twentieth centuries. In this they had certainly turned to a very fruitful source.

But perhaps it is wrong to stress the visionary, prophetic and cosmic nature of the Simplician writings too much, because it was the main fault of German literature in the seventeenth century to be always only too ready to point away from the real to the ideal, using every known rhetorical device for this purpose. As a result most of such writing is dead today, despite the recent revival of interest in allegorical writing and emblem books. Clearly it would be wrong to claim that the life Grimmelshausen was able to impart to the Simplician cycle derives from the half-concealed cosmic and astrological structure. The most obvious source of the novel's power lies in that simple but problematic quality most often associated with the picaresque, namely realism.[1] Needless to say critics and literary historians have found it far from easy to define the exact nature of Grimmelshausen's realism. It is certainly not sufficient to say that this novel is realistic because of the details it offers, e.g. of the tortures inflicted by the *soldateska* on the peasants, or of the particular articles of apparel which were worn on ceremonial occasions. A novel can as easily drown in details as it can come to life through them. In the non-picaresque novels which Grimmelshausen wrote he gave a mass of detail about high society and yet these remain completely stereotyped and dead, gathering dust in the libraries while his picaresque adventures are still read and enjoyed by generation after generation. Is it sufficient to equate realism with low life? Is low life more real than high? Are low-life characters more real than high-life characters? They would seem to be. However lacking they may be in personal psychology, individual emotion and consistent development figures like Courasche, Simplicius and Olivier seem so full of life they almost leap off the page. But perhaps the true essence of Grimmelshausen's realism lies in the difference between 'is' and 'ought', for he continuously seems to present the world as it is, and not as it ought to be according to the ideals of the age. Accordingly his world emerges as one in which life is an embittered and relentless struggle for

---

[1] The following discussion of Grimmelshausen's realism is based on F. H. T. Carr's Hull University M.A. thesis *Courasche and her Contemporaries* (1968). See especially Chap. 8b) in which Carr takes issue with R. Alewyn.

domination and survival. The individual is forced back constantly on to his or her own innate resources of intelligence and strength to avoid being dominated or destroyed. Does this imply a satirical approach to reality in Grimmelshausen? Certainly at least as far as the style is concerned it indicates a deeply ironical one. In Grimmelshausen there is an almost total lack of *milieu* description of the type common in works of nineteenth-century realism. Equally there is an almost total lack of personal, subjective experience.

On the other hand there is considerable concern always with the facts of life, with money, accommodation and self-preservation. This gives the novels a 'realistic' dimension that is totally absent from contemporary courtly and pastoral novels, whose protagonists are never disturbed by anything so mundane as economic problems. In order to stress the realism of his image of the world and of the society he depicts, Grimmelshausen carefully employs language that is typical of the colloquial language of his age. In this Carr has argued he is not the pure satirist (who forces his readers to reject the world he exposes in favour of some opposing ideal); on the contrary he is a burlesque writer, that is a realist who holds ideals but is also humorously aware of the gulf that separates the idealistic aspirations of man from the reality to which he is bound.[1] The burlesque writer is associated with 'low' literature because he stresses those aspects of reality which emphasise this truth of life. He shuns the heroic, the grand gesture, the sublime act, and stylistically all the phenomena which help to create an exalted style. Instead he prefers earthy, often sordid and repellent similes, racy cynical proverbs, generally crude and offensive vocabulary. To a considerable extent the burlesque style is a deliberate parody of the 'high' style associated with the courtly novel. This can become a means whereby the conventions of the high style are revealed as concealing the real forces in life. It exploits the comic possibilities in exaggerated proclamations of honour, virtue and sentiment by exposing them to a background of human savagery and degradation. The exalted ethos is thus contrasted with the struggle for power and pleasure which constitutes the ethos of the real world.

[1] These arguments are drawn from F. H. T. Carr's thesis, Chapter 9 'The problem of Grimmelshausen's Style': a) The burlesque style; b) The mock-heroic style; c) A comparison of the low and the high style.

The burlesque and the mock-heroic are complementary aspects of the author's unified view of life which is characterized by his ironic assault on convention. Although he could on occasion write in the more elaborate style of the Baroque, as certain passages even in *Simplicissimus* show, especially Book VI with its Allegory of Hell, he obviously found his own personal idiom in the pithy and racy style in which most of *Courasche* and much of *Simplicissimus* is written. Here too Grimmelshausen seems to have instinctively solved the language problem which baffled the greatest minds of the age. In the seventeenth century the German language was in a state of chaotic ferment and confusion which to a certain extent paralleled the political and religious confusions of the age. Yet Grimmelshausen broke through the jungle of learned discourse which characterized the gradual emergence of German as a literary language and found the vital force not in the rhetoric by which his contemporaries sought to raise German to the heights of art, but in the unbroken tradition of popular speech which Luther had successfully tapped more than a century before for his translation of the Bible. Not that Grimmelshausen was any more a man of the market place than Luther was. Both were extremely learned men steeped in humanistic and patristic literature, and yet they were able to exploit their feeling for the written word to create something that was fresh and lively and colourful no matter how many books they drew on. So successful indeed was Grimmelshausen in creating this feeling of immediacy and spontaneity which one associates with the Spanish picaresque that for a long time German critics insisted on treating Grimmelshausen as a naïve folk-poet writing simple folk-novels. They found it hard to believe that he had ever read a book and were convinced that he simply wrote as he felt, recording experiences from his own life. Recent research has gone almost to the other extreme and demonstrated that he was in fact a typically baroque writer in his lust for learning and his love of books. Just as his hero periodically withdraws from his adventures in the real world in order to read, so too clearly did Grimmelshausen almost literally devour books before incorporating them into his own picaresque epics. He had no hesitation in copying pages from other authors without any kind of acknowledgement, sometimes indeed whole chapters, stories and episodes were stolen from different sources and exploited for the next instalment of the Simplician saga. It would clearly be wrong to apply twentieth-century concepts of literary property and copyright to a seventeenth-century work, although here again there is a parallel between Grimmelshausen and Brecht, who was also prepared to take the material he wanted from wherever he found it. However, there is a problem for literary critics in the vast quantities of curious information and queer tales that Grimmelshausen misappropriated.[1] Passages which critics have admired for their realism and life turn out to have been taken from books. Other passages which have been admired for the way they demonstrate the author's imagination and creative talent have been traced to other sources.

It is not sufficient for the duped and angry critic to react by denouncing Grimmelshausen's plagiarism, his real task is to demonstrate how he transforms everything he steals by the magic of his touch. Grimmelshausen's realism is a distinct form of literary realism. He may appear to be registering events and incidents which have really happened, but only too often this is merely an illusion of actuality created by his artistry. Somehow he turns his reading into life and art into nature. The miracle is the manner in which Grimmelshausen by a few strokes changes what was dead and lifeless—for example Harsdörffer's versions of Spanish sources—into his own peculiar brand of vigorous German. The reader must constantly guard against the temptation to think of Grimmelshausen as naïve and untutored, and must be prepared to accept the fact that there is a literary source for practically everything he writes. Passages which seem most natural, personal and spontaneous are those which are most likely to have been taken from books he has read. His art lies in the concealment of art. His style may produce the effect of simplicity and naturalness but is in fact the product of high literary artistry in just the same way as his apparently shapeless narrative structures turn out to follow quite elaborate mathematical and indeed astrological patterns of a kind the baroque age loved.

The beauty of all this is that the reader who simply wants a good read does not need to worry about it. He is so immediately gripped by the feeling of personal engagement in the lives of these

---

[1] The problem of imitation and originality is the main burden of Weydt's latest book as the title *Nachahmung und Schöpfung* indicates.

rogues telling their life-stories that he tends to think of them as
real people and not as literary conventions. Yet here again the
absolute rightness in the choice of protagonists for the tales to be
told conceals the artistry of the author. It is the mark of the genius
to find the perfect protagonist as the crystallization point for what
he has to express. Goethe tried out many other titanic figures
before he at last found Faust. And Grimmelshausen certainly tried
his hand at almost every type of novel hero available to him before
tackling the *picaro* and the *picara*. But the figures he found and
refashioned in *Simplicissimus* proved absolutely ideal for his purposes, because he was able to merge the *picaro* with the traditional
German and indeed European figure of the Fool as the mirror of the
world. Once again he proves to be anything but a naïve and
spontaneous writer and instead turns out to be deeply involved in
the most complex problems of literary convention and derivation.
So, for example, ever since his cycle of Simplician stories appeared
readers have been reminded of 'Der reine Tor'—the pure fool
Parzival of Wolfram von Eschenbach. This enigmatic figure from
the Golden Age of medieval German literature seems a more
obvious source for Grimmelshausen's hero than any Spanish
picaro and yet how could this supposedly untutored German author
of the seventeenth century possibly have known a work written
in Middle High German and available only in manuscript form?
Parallels between Grimmelshausen's hero and Wolfram von
Eschenbach's *tumber*—the fool—seemed to indicate that he had
indeed taken over elements of the Parzival saga and fused this figure
with that of the Spanish *picaro* to make sacred simplicity personified
wander through the world like Parzival asking potentially fundamental questions. Yet there was a gap between apparent parallels
and definite contacts until recent researches were able to show that
it was possible, indeed probable, that Grimmelshausen did have
access to the *Parzival,* not it is true in manuscript, but in the
printed form which had been available since 1477.[1] Significantly,
however, Simplicissimus is neither simply the medieval German
figure nor the Spanish *picaro*. He is never merely the naïve hero.
Under Grimmelshausen's hands he has developed into someone
who is cunning and quick as well, now the butt, now the mocker

[1] See Günther Weydt: *Nachahmung und Schöpfung,* Section III, 3, pp. 202–16:
'Vom Parzival zum Simplicissimus'.

of the social spheres he passes through. This may still sound much like the Spanish *pícaro* yet at the same time there are some additional traits more familiar from the traditional figure of the fool as he developed in post-medieval Germany, as for example in Sebastian Brandt's *Ship of Fools* or in *Till Eulenspiegel* the chap-book hero with his merry pranks. In the simplest terms it was by his recognition of the potential of this many-faceted and traditional figure (whether Spanish or German) as a lively and amusing vehicle for all the things he wanted to express about his age that Grimmelshausen demonstrated his true genius. In the figure of the foolish *pícaro* hero Simplicissimus and to a somewhat lesser extent in that of the *pícara* heroine Courasche all the many strands come into focus to form the perfect first-person narrative.

Perhaps this explanation sounds too simple and the sophisticated reader may be tempted to demand of Grimmelshausen that he demonstrate his literary intention in writing such a cycle of tales in more explicitly aesthetic terms. And yet this far from aimless genius does declare his intentions in the very title of his *Simplicissimus*, and needless to say it proves to be a very ancient and well established aesthetic, namely *prodesse et delectare*. His aim is to be both useful and entertaining. Certainly in both *Simplicissimus* and *Courasche* he writes to amuse and there is no doubting his success in this intention. Both are extremely funny and this too, a funny German work of high literary value is something in the nature of a miracle. No one would wish to claim a monopoly in humour for the English or the French while repeating the widely held belief that the Germans have no sense of humour. Nevertheless, it must be admitted that there are not many great German comedies or comic novels. Hence the Simplician writings belong to a very select band indeed. The good humour in Grimmelshausen is constant and a deciding factor in the success of his work as a whole. However, the serious didactic purpose is no less apparent, though his ultimate goal may perhaps be more problematic. Grimmelshausen is constantly warning, teaching, preaching, exposing. There is generally a moral to be drawn from the tales he has to tell, though the interpretation given to the moral may vary greatly in particular cases. Nevertheless the didactic purpose can never be denied. And equally the framework of withdrawal from the world which is given to the five books of *Simplicissimus* inevitably casts a religious aura over the whole work. Grimmelshausen is clearly a serious religious writer with a serious religious intention. Yet significantly it is almost impossible to decide conclusively what the confessional colouring of his work is. In this respect he was perhaps typical of his time in that writing in a post-Reformation era about a war which was in part at least a war of religion, he not only demonstrated his own personal and deep religious feeling, but also attempted to rise above sectarian difference. Literature, as he demonstrates, is a means of bridging the sectarian gulf that separates man from man. Hence attempts by various critics to pin Grimmelshausen down as either Catholic or Protestant have inevitably proved futile. He is neither. Nor does he wish to deny all religion. Instead he seems to point forward to a religion of tolerance and true Christian humility. Here as elsewhere he gradually removes the conflict from the specific sphere of sectarian differences in one particular place at one particular time onto the much wider, almost cosmic level where the battle becomes that between the forces of light and darkness, good and evil in the world. His work remains firmly rooted in the real world of the Germany of the Thirty Years' War, but at the same time it gains enormously in range and depth and general application.

Yet however realistic, a work like *Simplicissimus* or *Courasche* remains a baroque work, and as in any work of German Baroque, whether it be a drama by Gryphius or a courtly novel by Zesen or Lohenstein, the central themes remain the same—life is a journey, life is a stage, life is an empty illusion. Hence not surprisingly masks figure prominently in the curious frontispiece and the motto given to the whole work is *Der Wahn betrügt*—the illusion deceives.[1] Appearances are deceptive, surface reality (= Schein) which, as has been seen, is presented in the most convincing manner, is as nought compared with real being (= Sein). In any baroque work the heroes or heroines are exposed to waves of intrigue, accidents, pirates, kidnappings, mistaken identities, all with the aim of testing their constancy. Temptations and threats of force succeed each other with fantastic speed, but always virtue triumphs in the end. Ups follow downs in rapid succession, yet however things turn out Fortuna rules the day, Fortuna a fickle goddess who can rush the hero to the top of the world one minute and plunge him

[1] Günther Weydt: op. cit., pp. 388–9, illustrations 18 and 19.

down to the depths the next. To some extent then the rapidly-changing fortunes of Simplicissimus and Courasche are in the picaresque tradition but at the same time their lives are remarkably similar to those of the heroes and heroines of all the courtly novels and plays of the time, though not played out at such a great height. And of course constancy is the proof of the pudding not just as something implicit in the text, but as something explicitly stated. Simplicius' mentor gives him three pieces of advice before passing away: (1) know thyself (2) avoid bad company (3) remain constant. We have seen how the Simplician writings as a kind of reflection on a mis-spent life are at least an attempt at self-knowledge. Equally we have seen how Simplicissimus largely fails to avoid bad company, allowing the reader to draw his own conclusions from his failure. So too in view of all the myriad transformations Simplicissimus passes through it is left up to the reader to decide the extent to which Simplicius is successful in remaining constant.

Baroque in another sense is the mass of curious information that Grimmelshausen, like his contemporaries, loved to pack into his novels. In a way this was a dangerous practice, for many a book of the seventeenth century never survived the surfeit of strange material it was expected to carry. Grimmelshausen, as has been seen, somehow managed to transform the pickings from his vast reading into sources of literary life. One such source which must be mentioned as a feature of Grimmelshausen's work is the erotic. This is undoubtedly a source of great vigour for his novels. It was, of course, also a feature of nearly all baroque writing in German, which loved to demonstrate the close links between spiritual and sensual love. Writers of the time were only too ready to contrast the longings of the spirit with the lusts of the flesh, hence it is not surprising that this aspect has such an important part to play in all the Simplician writings.

Courasche's whole amorous life is scandalous to say the least, and apparently a deliberate contrast to that of Simplicissimus, whose life is a progression from the ignorant bliss of the holy idiot to the conscious bliss of the man who wittingly withdraws from the world's temptations. However, on the way to that stage Simplicius too demonstrates his prowess as a great lover, at one time making his way to the very Mount of Venus, namely Paris, where as the 'Beau Alman', he becomes a kind of willing stallion for all the lustful ladies that city is famous for. Often the erotic is combined with the humorous as, for example, in the earlier incident when the ignorant simpleton first experiences a dance. Not knowing what it means he believes Herzbruder who tells him that the dancers are trying to smash through the floor and is so terrified that he fills his breeches and creates a smell. As a punishment for the disturbance he causes he is locked in a goose pen which soon proves to be a favourite spot for amorous adventures, for the next thing Simplicius knows is that a 'goose' and a 'gander' have sneaked into the darkened little room. Once again he has no idea of what the pair are about, although he can hear the lady complain about the smell and the man reply in the excessively flowery language of such occasions:

> To be sure, lovely lady, my heart is most assuredly deeply distressed that Fortuna has not favoured us with a more noble place to enjoy the fruits of our love. But this notwithstanding I do assure my lady that her gracious presence renders this despicable corner more delightful than the very bliss of paradise itself.

(Bk. II, Chap. I)

This is followed by a great deal of kissing and writhing which Simplicius entirely fails to comprehend, so that when the whole place begins to creak and the woman looks as if she is suffering bodily harm he is convinced that these must be some of the same people who were trying to kick the dance-floor in and that he is a witness to a murder. He rushes from the room screaming, carefully locking the pair in as he leaves. So it comes about that Simplicissimus in his ignorance first observes the act of love—or, as he puts it, this was his first wedding, though he had not been exactly an invited guest.

This incident is typical of the humorous treatment Grimmelshausen affords his lively erotic material. An even more famous example is to be found in the life story of Simplicissimus' female counterpart when it turns out that her very name, Courage, has sexual overtones.[1] The lady, it must be remembered, tells her own

---

[1] The following passages are quoted from the Hiller-Osborne translation (Lincoln, Nebraska 1965), pp. 43–45. The heading at the top of the Chapter 3, with its

story. Here she looks back to the time when she was still a virgin, dressed as a man and acting as a servant to a dashing captain of horse. After a successful battle she gets into a fight with a common soldier who rouses her wrath by a very dirty trick:

> Both of us came to cursewords, from cursewords to blows, and from blows to scuffling and wrestling, during which work my adversary whisked his hand inside my trousers to seize me by that equipment which I, after all, did not possess, which futile but murderous hold vexed me much more than if he had not found himself empty-handed.

After winning the fight and mutilating the soldier who had un-wittingly uncovered the secret of her sex she has to tell her captain of horse the story and explain why she has thrashed her adversary so horribly:

> 'Because he made a grab for my *courage*, which place no man's hands have touched.' (For I wished to express myself delicately and did not want to call it by as crude a name as the Suabians . . .).

Needless to say the dashing young captain is delighted and amused and the incident closes with Courasche at last happily losing her virginity to him:

> He could not but laugh at how I had described with a new name many of the colors which were to be found on my escutcheon. He consoled me most kindly and promised with high-flown words to protect my honor like his own life; but with his deeds he soon showed that he would be the first to rob me of my maidenhead; and I myself liked his unchaste groping better than his honorable promises; however, I defended myself vali-antly; not, of course, to escape him or to flee his lustful advances, but to really excite him and to make him even more lustful; and the trick succeeded so well in every way that I allowed nothing to happen till he promised, or might the devil fetch him, to wed me, despite the fact that I could well imagine that he had no more intention of keeping his promise than of cutting his own throat.

Grimmelshausen, however, is never merely funny or entertaining,

---

clever word play, gives a good indication of the overall humorous tone of the narrative: 'While serving with a resolute captain of horse Janco exchanges his noble hymen for the nomen Courage'.

his aim is always to be 'useful' as well. To this end, as has been seen, he was prepared to draw on a vast range of sources varying from *Parzival* through the chap-books, folk-tales, patristic sources on the lives of the saints to guides to the stars. But he was essentially writing a 'popular' novel and for this the most important influences were unquestionably Spanish. Of the many Spanish sources he turned to perhaps the title of the *Courasche* novel gives the best clue, for he called it the story of the *Landstörtzerin Courasche*. The word *Landstörtzer* was that used by Aegidius Albertinus for his translation in 1615 of the picaresque novel *Guzmán de Alfarache*. There are, in other words, clear links between this *Landstörtzer* and *Simplicissimus*.[1] The hero of Albertinus' work is

> a reformed rogue who sets down the story of his disreputable life with much detail but little art. He describes his humble birth, his childhood, his initiation into the guild of professional thieves, and the many exploits in which he engages before his repentance in old age. At intervals throughout the story the reader is reminded that this account of Guzmán's rogueries is intended as a warning, to beware of bad company and to resist the temptations of the wicked world.[2]

Indeed the German version is far more moral than the Spanish, for Albertinus was Jesuit-trained and his interests were religious rather than literary. Hence he expanded the moral digressions already present to some extent in his Spanish source and added new digressions of his own. His narrative remains racy and amusing, but the didactic intention is now distinctly more prominent. By the end of his German version in three volumes, which was completed by another hand, the hero is converted to the religious life, makes a pilgrimage to the Holy Land and subsequently withdraws from the world to become a hermit. This is very close indeed to the pattern of *Simplicissimus*.

Once again Grimmelshausen seems about to be proven guilty of plagiarism. He does indeed seem to have stolen the basic structure for his *Simplicissimus* from *Guzmán* by way of Albertinus. But all this was long before the days of copyright and the inviolability of

[1] Hans Gerd Rötzer: *Picaro—Landstörtzer—Simplicius* (Darmstadt 1972).
[2] K. G. Knight: 'Grimmelshausen's *Simplicissimus*—a popular baroque novel' in *Periods in German Literature*, ed. J. M. Ritchie (London 1969), Vol. II, p. 6.

literary property. Indeed it has been argued that Grimmelshausen was simply dealing in what was by that time common property. It has been pointed out for example that there was no need to go to Spain for a picaresque model, he could equally well have turned to a French one and in particular to Charles Sorel's *Histoire Comique de Francion*.[1] There are certainly parallels between Grimmelshausen's work and this French novel and it seems possible, indeed probable, that he did exploit it for his own purpose. Yet however close the similarities, there are differences as well which allow for a defence of Grimmelshausen against the perpetual charge of plagiarism. It is Heselhaus' contention in particular that Grimmelshausen never simply took over the French model unchanged any more than he simply plagiarised Spanish sources. On the contrary he deserves the credit for having created in Simplicissimus a native German equivalent to the Spanish or French hero, a German hero in a German setting! The name Francion for example indicates a frank, open person. To a certain extent this is also descriptive of the German hero, but Grimmelshausen has moved beyond frankness to simplicity because it offered more potential for development. In other words Grimmelshausen improved upon his French model by giving far more than either his French or his Spanish sources. His hero is not really characterized by that cynical brand of realism in the description of the customs of the age which one associates with the traditional picaresque hero. Instead his Simplicissimus is far more complex than, for example, Francion who never worries, never thinks and never changes. Simplicissimus has the same freedom of the spirit and the same freedom of movement of the conventional Francion figure, but far from being untouched by events he seems constantly deepened by them. In effect the contemporary baroque theme of *nosce te ipsum* which Grimmelshausen made a fundamental part of his tale develops into an almost Faustian 'spiritual unrest'—hence his novel attains a metaphysical-religious dimension which goes far beyond anything that any of his picaresque sources had to offer. In arguing this way it may appear that Heselhaus is reading too much into the text from over-eagerness to rescue Grimmelshausen from the odium of being a mere plagiarist. However, it is fair enough to stress the tale's

[1] Clemens Heselhaus: 'Der abenteuerliche Simplicissimus' in *Der deutsche Roman*, ed. Benno v. Wiese (Düsseldorf 1963), Bd. I, p. 15ff.

German qualities. And indeed as another critic K. G. Knight has pointed out, Grimmelshausen did have a German precursor who had succeeded in producing 'a native equivalent to the picaresque novel with a German hero in a German setting'. This was the Alsatian H. M. Moscherosch whom he is known to have read. Moscherosch's main work follows the general pattern of the soldier's life in the Thirty Years' War. Like Simplicissimus his hero is not always a willing participant in the hostilities which he too describes with incredible realism of detail, and like Simplicissimus he reaches the point of repentance in the end, renounces all his sinful ways and swears to lead a better life. In effect, as Professor Knight has pointed out, Moscherosch's *Soldier's Life* like *Guzmán* is basically 'an autobiography with a moral':

> The chronicle of the hero's mis-spent life is followed by an account of his conversion and reform like the testimony of repentant sinners at a revivalist meeting of certain modern sects. And in the picaresque novel the two elements—the wicked life and the exemplary conversion—are linked in the person of the hero who has passed through both experiences.[1]

This is a fair point and it is true too that both Albertinus and Moscherosch had difficulty in combining the two elements, the wicked life and the necessary conversion. Hence there tended to be a break not only in their narrative flow but also in their stylistic levels between the diverting low-life pranks and the elevating Christian moral. Professor Knight argues that Grimmelshausen succeeded where his predecessors failed in bridging the gulf between these two parts. There are now no authorial intrusions to point the moral; instead it is Simplicissimus himself who combines the double perspective by both telling the story of his life with all the zest and zeal of personal involvement and commenting on his own follies where necessary. Needless to say it is also the constant presence of this narrator which gives the whole narrative both the warm humour and the unfailing irony which all precursors lack.

In discussing *Simplicius Simplicissimus* in English one is clearly talking about a book or a series of books of which few non-Germans will ever have heard. Inside the German-speaking lands this may be considered one of the greatest novels ever written and as has

[1] Op. cit., p. 7.

been seen, there is some justification for such a judgement, but it still remains unknown and unread elsewhere. Until fairly recently this might also have been true of the seventh book of the Simplician cycle, but since the international success of Brecht's play *Mother Courage* all this has changed. Not surprisingly there have been two translations of the *Landstörtzerin Courasche* into English in the last few years, translations inspired more by an interest in Brecht's sources than by any desire to know more about seventeenth-century German literature. That this is so is evidenced by the fact that the great Brecht propagandist Eric Bentley is called upon to write the preface to one of them.[1] In fact, however, even the most cursory comparison of Brecht's play with the novel immediately reveals that they are almost entirely different. Brecht has adopted the *pícara* figure but altered everything else. In the context of the plagiarism/originality problem with which one is constantly faced when dealing with Grimmelshausen it is an interesting exercise in 'originality' to examine Brecht's treatment of the material he stole from Grimmelshausen.

Compared with *Simplicius Simplicissimus, Courage the Adventuress,* or *The Runagate Courage,* as the newest translation calls it, is a very short book. Once again one is dealing with an autobiography though this time the moral is not quite so apparent, for this is the autobiography of a harlot whom Simplicius met at a spa or watering-place, a favourite literary locale for amorous dallyings. Unlike Brecht's character she is never a mother. Significantly despite all her rampant sexual activity she always remains barren. And when she tells the story of her adventurous and dissolute life it is for the sole purpose of taking revenge on Simplicius the lover who slighted her. The title of her story, *Trutz Simplex* reads in full as follows:

To spite Simplex or the detailed and wondorously strange life history of the archfraud and runagate Courage, how she first was the wife of a captain of horse; afterwards the wife of a captain of infantry, further the wife of a sutler, the wife of a musketeer, and finally the wife of a gypsy. Expertly carried out and excellently described and just as entertaining, agreeable, and profitable to contemplate as Simplicissimus himself. All of it dictated

[1] *The Runagate Courage,* translated by Robert L. Hiller and John C. Osborne, preface (v–viii) by Eric Bentley (Univ. Nebraska Press, Lincoln, Nebraska 1965).

by the person of Courage herself for the displeasure and disgust
of the well known Simplicissimus directly to the author who this
time calls himself Philarchus Grossus of Trommenheim at Griffs-
berg etc. Printed in Utopia by Felix Stratiot.

The reason for the anger which inspires her to tell her story is that
Simplicissimus not only enjoyed her favours but boasted of it to
all the world while in addition exposing her to public ridicule.
He shot blanks at her from a pistol, and then using a syringe full of
blood made her believe she had been wounded. She then showed
herself not only to the leech who was supposed to bandage her but
to the people of Sauerbrunnen who afterwards pointed her out in
the streets, sang a song about the incident, mocked her and forced
her to leave. By way of retaliation she dresses up her maid's baby
in rich clothes and leaves it on the doorstep of Simplicissimus who
is now a married man, pretending it is the child of their love-
making. In other words she manages to make the 'simpleton'
believe that she, a barren woman, had borne a child although she
was already beyond the age of child-bearing when she had her
affair with him. In the end Fortune smiles upon Simplex as always,
because it turns out that he had been having a secret affair with
Courage's maid. Hence the child proves to be his son after all. So
the foiler is foiled. The tale is a typically baroque one of mistaken
identities, changing relationships and startling twists of fate told
throughout with Grimmelshausen's characteristic humour.

In a sense the lengthy title to the Courage novel with its
catalogue of her constantly changing rôles is a pointer to the
protean nature of Grimmelshausen's novels, protean that is in the
sense that the protagonists are constantly changing shape and
appearance.[1] Hence Simplex, who is revealed at the end as an
abandoned princeling, starts life as a simple peasant lad in the
simplest of peasant garb. He then becomes an assistant to a hermit
and dresses as would be expected of one living in the wilderness.
When he goes out into the world he is dressed in fool's clothing by
the world and acts accordingly. At the height of his career he is the
Huntsman of Soest and famous for his suit of Lincoln Green. When

---

[1] B. L. Spahr: 'Protean Stability in the Baroque Novel,' *GR* XL (1965) 253–60.
See also A. Jolles: 'Die literarischen Travestien: Ritter-Hirt-Schelm' in *Pikarische
Welt: Schriften zum europäischen Schelmenroman*, ed. Helmut Heidenreich (Darm-
stadt 1969), pp. 101–18.

Fortuna turns against him he drops down the social scale and ends up a marauder in rags before climbing up once more to end his life as a peasant and finally as a hermit. Having completed his passage through all the pleasures and pains the world has to offer he turns his back on them all. He has progressed from *sancta simplicitas* to a kind of learned simplicity which is given appropriate expression by the famous farewell to the world speech taken by Grimmelshausen from Bishop Guevara.[1] Significantly perhaps, the German picaresque tale finishes on a Spanish note. Taken as a whole the novel has not presented a constant *pícaro* figure but rather one exposed to a series of protean changes culminating in the appropriate moral. Similarly *Courage the Adventuress* also finishes with a postscript conveying almost too late, it would seem, the moral to be drawn from her dissolute life:

Addendum of the Author

Now for this reason then, you chaste youths, you honorable widowers, and even you married men who have hitherto avoided these dangerous *chimeris*, eluded these terrible medusas, stopped your ears against these cursed sirens and forsworn these unfathomable and bottomless *belidibus*, or at least withstood them by fleeing, let these *Lupas* not henceforth enchant you in the future; for one thing is certain: That there is nought else to be expected from loving whores than all manner of uncleanness, shame, ridicule, poverty, and misery, and worst of all a bad conscience too. Only when it is too late does one realize what one had in them, how nasty they are, how vile, how lice-ridden, scabby, unclean, stinking both of breath and of their whole body, how full of French disease within and full of pustulent sores without; so that in the end one must, in his own heart, be ashamed of it and, oft times, much too late, deplore it.

Consideration of the endings of the two deliberately contrasting works *Simplicissimus* and *Courasche* has led to some discussion of their relevant structures. *Simplicissimus*, by reason of its spiritually uplifting ending, has always naturally been considered to indicate an ascending structure. *Courasche* on the other hand needs to have an author's moral tacked on at the end of her own account of her

[1] Günther Weydt: 'Weltklage und Lebensrückblick bei Guevara, Albertinus und Grimmelshausen', *Nachahmung und Schöpfung*, pp. 216–40.

life. She herself shows little or no remorse or repentance and seems to be punished accordingly. She starts off reasonably high and seems gradually to sink lower and lower. It is therefore natural to consider her story as an account of a descending life. Certainly the novel is as protean as *Simplicissimus* for she too is constantly changing appearances and social position, although the only part of her life in which Brecht was interested was her period of commercial activity as a sutler-woman or vivandière. However, unlike other heroes of picaresque novels who proceed from one adventure to the next without change or development of character, Courage does change under the influence of experience. As with Simplicissimus there is an element of self-awareness that adds warmth, humour and irony to what might otherwise be a rather unpleasant story. So in the early part of the novel she is not the evil and spiteful woman she later appears to be. She is a naturally lustful woman who right from the start says yes to war and yes to love. But at the same time through her life-story as she tells it the real forces at work in her time are revealed, all her fundamental attitudes and beliefs are exposed to view. All life she shows is war, and love too, which is her métier, is war in another guise. Hence her story is not merely a petty grievance against one man Simplex; the novel develops a much wider frame of reference just as *Simplicius Simplicissimus* does, until the private squabble has become a cosmic battle of the sexes. She is a Renaissance virago, an Amazon, better in battle than the men, and better in love than the men! She is in fact a magnificent beast, and *bestia* is one of Grimmelshausen's favourite words. Chapter 9 of *Simplicissimus*, for example, has the heading 'How Simplicius changed from a *bestia* to a Christian'. Whether Courage ever becomes a good Christian is extremely problematic, for in this sphere too she is the polar opposite of the man she loves to hate. But if she remains a beast, then she is a magnificent beast. 'Mulier non homo' was one of the popular slogans of the time. A woman is not a man, indeed perhaps a woman is not human! But a woman like Courage shows herself supremely capable of surviving all the horrors to which a senseless and inscrutable fate exposes her. This is perhaps the main feature of her persona that Brecht captured. In his play too the structure seems to be a descending one. The audience is made to see Courage going downhill whoever much the circular motion of the cart may suggest that her struggle will be unending. But the main thing is that she never gives up, she never stops struggling and by the end the audience cannot help admiring her courage and fortitude. Brecht was, of course, very disturbed by this—he wanted the audience to see the error of her ways even if she remained blind. But admiration for the Niobe figure triumphed over the moral. In Grimmelshausen's version, of course, she is not a mother and so does not suffer the loss of her own children as a result of her efforts to make a living out of war. She is corrupt and wicked, she has wild and insatiable appetites for men and wealth and she is full of avarice and envy. And yet at the end of it all as in Brecht's play one cannot help admiring this woman, perhaps because in an age of hypocrisy and false appearances she never pretends to be anything other than she is. She is natural and open and, of course, every utterance she makes is deeply ironic and very funny. Her very name is funny. As has been seen, it had undoubted sexual connotations; it is also deeply appropriate for one who has so much real guts, vitality and sheer common sense. This then is how she is remembered, not as the broken woman at the end of a sinful life but as one whose life seems even more exemplary than that of the hermit Simplicissimus.

Grimmelshausen was so much of a plagiarist that as with Simplicissimus one is tempted to look for literary models for such a vital figure. Generally speaking, there is more speculation than fact about this, but on the whole it seems probable that a Spanish source may have helped Grimmelshausen when he came to write his tale of the *pícara*.[1] It is considered unlikely that *Courage the Adventuress* owes much to Úbeda's *Pícara Justina* (1605) although Grimmelshausen may have been familiar with the German translation of that work.[2] On the whole it seems most probable that the intermediary in this case was Harsdörffer who by his translations of Spanish tales had already provided so much of the material to be found in *Simplicissimus*. In a sense Grimmelshausen was following the normal pattern of any baroque writer. He had already tried his hand at every type of novel available to him at the time. He had

[1] J. A. van Praag: 'Die Schelmin in der spanischen Literatur' in *Pikarische Welt*, pp. 147–64.
[2] ' "La picaresca": Gedanken zu López de Ubedas *La picara Justina*' in *Pikarische Welt*, pp. 412–37.

written courtly novels, pastoral novels, biblical novels, novels of high life, novels of low life, calendar tales, etc. Of these *Simplicissimus* had proved the most successful. What more natural than that, having done the novel of the *pícaro* he should also do the novel of the *pícara*? It was the accepted practice of the time to write a poem on one theme and immediately contrast it with its opposite: beauty-ugliness, youth-age, constancy-inconstancy, good-evil. This is what he appears to be doing with the contrasting figures of Simplex and Courasche, simple man and cunning woman, though being a truly baroque writer he was not averse to doing both at the same time. Hence as has been repeatedly observed, figures like Courasche are both sexes at once, they are hermaphrodites who move freely between the sexes, now male, now female, now active, now passive. Contemporary books loved to show illustrations of hermaphroditic monsters—indeed, something of this seems to have entered into the famous grotesque frontispiece to the whole Simplician cycle.[1]

Much has been spoken here about miracles in connection with Grimmelshausen. The greatest miracle of all is that his work is still so much alive when nearly everything else from the literature of seventeenth-century Germany has died or retained at most historical interest. Perhaps this life is largely due to the picaresque mode he adopted. Whatever the reason, *Simplicissimus* is a major masterpiece and *Courage the Adventuress* is a minor one. Naturally the picaresque mode exercised considerable influence on later German writers, but the only masterpiece which can be shown to have benefited directly from this influence was Eichendorff's *Taugenichts*.[2] Eichendorff's charming tale has indeed been described as the '*Simplicissimus* of Romanticism'. There are other odd examples of the picaresque in later periods of German literature, but it was not until the twentieth century that it really came to life again. Brecht's work is not only full of picaresque anti-heroes—his whole life seems picaresque. Thomas Mann's *Felix Krull* in this vein is generally singled out as his most amusing and entertaining work, and in more recent years novels like Günther Graß' *Tin Drum* have shown a distinct predilection not only for the episodic picaresque structure but even for the kind of seventeenth-century language in

[1] Günther Weydt: op. cit., p. 385: 'Hermaphrodit'.
[2] Eichendorff's *Aus dem Leben eines Taugenichts*, ed. J. M. Ritchie (London 1970).

which *Simplicissimus* is couched. There has even been a novel called *Simplicius 45* which clearly harks back to the great work. Hence it can be said that although Grimmelshausen's Simplician Cycle did not inspire any immediate line of succession, nevertheless it did establish a tradition which never died and which is bearing fruit to this day.

BIBLIOGRAPHY

Texts

GRIMMELSHAUSEN, H. J. C. von: *The Adventurous Simplicissimus being the description of the life of a strange vagabond named Melchior Sternfels von Fuchsaim written in German . . . and now for the first time done into English* (by A. T. S. G.), (London 1912).
— *The Adventurous Simplicissimus*, trans. A. T. S. Goodrich (Univ. Nebraska Press, Lincoln, Nebraska 1962).
— *The Adventures of a Simpleton*, trans. W. Wallich (London 1962). A much abridged and bowdlerized version.
— *Simplicius Simplicissimus*, trans. H. Weissenborn and L. Macdonald (London 1964).
— *Simplicius Simplicissimus*, trans. G. Schulz-Behrend (Indianapolis, New York and Kansas City 1965).
— *Courage the Adventuress, and the False Messiah*, trans. and intro. H. Speier (Princeton U.P., Princeton (N.J.) 1964).
— *The Runagate Courage*, trans. Robert L. Hiller and John C. Osborne (Univ. Nebraska Press, Lincoln, Nebraska 1965).

Critical Works

GENERAL:
Faber du Faur, Curt von: *German Baroque Literature; a catalogue of the collection in the Yale University Library* (Yale U.P., New Haven 1958).
Heidenreich, H. (ed.): *Pikarische Welt: Schriften zum europäischen Schelmenroman* (Darmstadt 1969).
Spahr, B. L.: 'Protean Stability in the Baroque Novel,' *GR* XL (1965) 253–60.

GRIMMELSHAUSEN, H. J. C. von:
Carr, F. H. T.: *Courasche and her Contemporaries; a contribution to the study of the novel in Germany in the seventeenth century*, M.A. thesis, University of Hull (1968).
Haynes, Kenneth C.: *Grimmelshausen* (St. Andrews University Publication No. XXXIV, Oxford U.P. 1932).

Heselhaus, C.: 'Grimmelshausen, Der abenteuerliche Simplicissimus,' in *Der deutsche Roman*, ed. Benno v. Wiese (Düsseldorf 1963), Bd. I, pp. 15–63.

Jacobsen, J. J.: 'The Culpable Male: Grimmelshausen on women,' *GQ* XXXIX, ii (1966) 149–61.

Jacobsen, J. J.: 'A Defense of Grimmelshausen's Courasche,' *GQ* XLI, i (1968) 42–54.

Klingebiel, E.: *Die Olivier-Handlung im 'Simplicius Simplicissimus': ein Beitrag zur Grimmelshausenforschung*. Dissertation (Kiel 1956).

Knight, K. G.: 'Grimmelshausen's *Simplicissimus*—a popular baroque novel,' in *Periods in German Literature*, ed. J. M. Ritchie (London 1969), Vol. II, pp. 3–20.

Rötzer, H. G.: *Picaro—Landstörtzer—Simplicius: Studien zum niederen Roman in Spanien und Deutschland* (Darmstadt 1972).

Scholte, J. H.: *Der Simplicissimus und sein Dichter: gesammelte Aufsätze* (Tübingen 1950).

Weydt, Günther: 'Adjeu Welt: Weltklage und Lebensrückblick bei Guevara, Albertinus und Grimmelshausen,' *Neophilologus* XLVI (1962) 105–25.

Weydt, Günther: *Nachahmung und Schöpfung im Barock: Studien um Grimmelshausen* (Bern 1968).

Weydt, Günther (ed.): *Der Simplicissimusdichter und sein Werk* (Darmstadt 1969).

MOSCHEROSCH, H. M.:

Knight, K. G.: 'Moscherosch's Soldatenleben,' *GLL* VII (1953) 48–55.

Knight, K. G.: 'H. M. Moscherosch—an early baroque satirist's view on life,' *MLR* XLIX (1954) 29–45.

J. A. MICHIE

The Unity of *Moll Flanders*

A T FIRST SIGHT DEFOE'S MOLL FLANDERS MAY NOT
seem to possess much coherence of theme or action. The
apparently flat, episodic nature of the narrative has left many
readers with the impression that Moll herself is the only immediately discernible principle of unity in the book. The incidents are
levelled out on a straight narrative plane, observes Mark Schorer.[1]
Moll dominates the book, says E. M. Forster; she stands alone
'like a tree in a park'.[2] The question arises, however, whether the
details of the story are indeed merely circumstantial or yield a
definable thematic and structural coherence. Professor Sutherland,
in his excellent study, holds the view that in Defoe's two Plague
books and in the first part of *Robinson Crusoe* 'the very circumstances
impose a certain order on the narrative', but that in his other
fictitious works Defoe is 'apt to be merely episodic; event follows
event in a natural time sequence, and no other unity is aimed at
than that which is given by the hero or heroine'.[3] Professor Watt,
in his influential work, *The Rise of the Novel*,[4] finds no structural
control of the materials in *Moll Flanders*. On the issue of whether or
not there is an ironic remove, in any large sense, between Moll and
her creator, he is prepared to concede that there are some local
examples of conscious irony, as when little Moll prophetically
announces that when she grows up she will be a gentlewoman like
the town whore who does not have any housework to do and is
called 'madam'. But these ironic passages, Watt argues, do not

[1] *Moll Flanders*, Modern Library College Edition (New York 1950), p. xii, from
the Introduction by Mark Schorer.
[2] E. M. Forster: *Aspects of the Novel* (New York 1927), p. 88.
[3] James Sutherland: *Defoe* (2nd edition, London 1950), p. 241.
[4] Ian Watt: *The Rise of the Novel* (London 1957), p. 104.

form part of a comprehensive pattern. Most of them, he maintains, are properly to be regarded as accidents, 'produced by the random application of narrative authenticity to conflicts in Defoe's social and moral and religious world, accidents which unwittingly reveal to us the serious discrepancies in his system of values . . . *Moll Flanders* is undoubtedly an ironic object, but it is not a work of irony'. One would not, of course, lightly dissent from such authoritative criticism, but a close reading of Defoe does not leave one disposed to accept uncritically or unreservedly the use of words like 'random', 'accidents' and 'unwittingly'. There is a greater degree of conscious literary art in this novel than such terms would suggest. The aim of this paper is to try to demonstrate that *Moll Flanders* has a stronger claim to structural unity, involving theme, character and action, than has hitherto been acknowledged.

On the level of plot, the general pattern of events can be interpreted as one which develops the opening scenes, every major episode being a logical expression of Moll's persistent desire to become a gentlewoman, a desire which is prefigured in her first dialogues with the nurse. Below this surface logic of outward action there is, secondly, a logic of spiritual change within the protagonist. The book has a coherence to be found in the gradual unfolding of the inward states of Moll's character. Defoe is concerned with the processes of spiritual change as well as with the overt actions by which these processes are revealed. He is interested not simply in action—a fact which has always been recognized and indeed received a disproportionate amount of critical, not to say censorious, emphasis—but also in being and becoming—an aspect of his work which has been relatively neglected by the majority of critics. To defend the novel's unity on only one of these levels is, however well intentioned, to do it a disservice, for this is to rob it of its richness. To concentrate on its outward social and economic aspects at the cost of its inner meaning is to sacrifice the fable for the story. Equally, to maintain, as does George Starr,[1] that 'a conventional pattern of spiritual decay supplies' a degree of 'thematic coherence despite any amount of incoherence in the outward narrative', whilst admitting that 'some portions of the narrative are not spiritualized at all', is unsatisfactory since 'the outward

[1] George Starr: *Defoe and Spiritual Autobiography* (Princeton U.P. 1965), chapter IV, an excellent book to which I am greatly indebted.

narrative' accounts for at least half the book. What is needed, in order to bring out the deeper unity of the novel, is a reconciliation of these approaches, the union of the story of Moll's aspirations to middle-class gentility with the moral fable of what became of her in the process of striving towards that end.

'It isn't difficult to be a country gentleman's wife . . . I think I could be a good woman if I had five thousand a year.' The thought which occurred to Thackeray's Rebecca might well have struck a responsive chord in Moll Flanders. Not that she was capable of any sustained flight of abstract speculation on the relation of economics to morality. All that she wants from life, she says, is 'to be placed in a settled way of living'. But, like everything else about Moll, the phrase is not susceptible of simple interpretation. To understand her and her career involves an understanding of what precisely she means by 'a settled way of living' and the kind of security she desires.

What Defoe portrays in Moll's early life is the plight of an unfortunate girl ('the offspring of debauchery and vice') who, conscious of her beauty and brains, comes to aspire to a more genteel life than the drudgery of going out to service, the usual fate of girls in her class and circumstances. Moll's aspirations, though not of course the means of attaining them, are to a large extent the result of her education. Like some of Defoe's other main characters, she is orphaned at an early age, for her mother is transported to the plantations as a convicted thief. At the age of about two she is deserted by a band of wandering gypsies in Colchester, where she is placed by the magistrate of the town under the care of a nurse in the local orphanage. This woman had previously lived in 'good fashion', and Moll is 'brought up as mannerly as if (she) had been at the dancing school'. Moll takes instinctively to this fashionable education and her first experience of fear is at the age of eight, when she is 'terrified' at the news that the magistrates had ordered her to 'go to service'. Her fear springs from the realization that such a prospect will offer her little beyond running errands or being 'a drudge to some cookmaid'. It is a threat to the taste for fashionable living which she has imbibed from her teacher. 'What! would you be a gentlewoman?' asks the teacher incredulously of the tearful girl; and, when Moll, in all innocence, replies 'Yes', the absurdity of so pretentious an aspiration sets her 'a-laughing'. 'As you may be sure it would,' adds Moll the narrator of her memoirs, with the bitterness of hindsight.

'Well, madam, forsooth,' says she, gibing at me, 'you would be a gentlewoman; and how will you come to be a gentlewoman? What! will you do it by your fingers' ends?' 'Yes,' says I again, very innocently. 'Why, what can you earn,' says she; 'what can you get a day at your work?' 'Threepence,' said I, 'when I spin, and fourpence when I work plain work.' 'Alas! poor gentlewoman,' said she again, laughing, 'what will that do for thee?'

From this initial action Moll charts the course of her life. Innocent, at this stage, of what the world understands by the term, she will learn in time what it means to be a gentlewoman.

Meanwhile her ambitions in this direction become known to the mayor and his family, who are vastly amused. The mayoress is sufficiently curious to wish to meet 'the little lass that is to be a gentlewoman'. Moll, though she is quite vague on the subject, is nevertheless encouraged by all the gratifying fuss which people begin to make over her to stick to her aim in life. For one thing, she finds that it pays. She is rewarded with flattery and money by the mayoress. The pattern of flattery and reward is repeated when she is visited by the mayoress's daughters. So she holds fast to her ambition. But she is puzzled. It seems to her that the towns-people 'meant one sort of thing by the word gentlewoman, and I meant quite another'. All she wants at this stage is the means to support herself and not to have to go out to service, but they think she 'meant to live great and high'. Only gradually does Moll's teacher realize what she means by the term:

My old tutoress began to understand what I meant by being a gentlewoman, and it was no more than to be able to get my bread by my own work; and at last she asked me whether it was not so.

I told her, yes, and insisted on it, that to do so was to be a gentlewoman; 'for,' says I, 'there is such a one,' naming a woman that mended lace and washed the ladies' laced heads; 'she,' says I, 'is a gentlewoman, and they call her madam.'

'Poor child,' says my good old nurse, 'you may soon be such a gentlewoman as that, for she is a person of ill fame, and has had two bastards.'

I did not understand anything of that; but I answered, 'I am sure they call her madam, and she does not go to service nor do housework'; and therefore I insisted that she was a gentlewoman, and I would be such a gentlewoman as that.

The scene is ironic, of course, in a double sense, skilfully spotlighting the young girl's innocence on the subject of gentility and at the same time foreshadowing her later, far-from-innocent, career.

Moll's social education is significantly developed by her association with ladies in the town. She receives fine cast-off clothes from them. One of them invites her to spend a week with her daughters at her home. As a result of this exposure to fashionable living in the home of a lady, Moll at fourteen acquires a more sophisticated concept of what it means to be a gentlewoman. But, as her tutoress predicts, such experience will do her more harm than good. Amused by her presumption, the ladies humour her, flatter her vanity, and assure her she may indeed become a gentlewoman. Every time they see her they give her money, thus reinforcing by coin the social gap while encouraging her ambitions.

It is worth noting, since Defoe's structural skill has not always been appreciated, that it is precisely at this point, when Moll feels the strongest attraction to the genteel way of life which she has been imitating for years by her clothes and manners, that her old teacher and protectress dies suddenly. Once again Moll is seized with fear, that fear for the future which is so often to determine her conduct. Fortunately—or so it seems at the time—she is taken into the home of a wealthy family, where she is afforded every opportunity to nourish her aspirations to gentility. As a companion to the daughters of the household, she is given lessons in dancing, French, music, and writing. In these she soon becomes more proficient than the authentic gentlewomen. Defoe contrasts sharply the difference between the natural attributes of beauty and brains evident in Moll and the artificial advantages of birth and position enjoyed by the daughters.

Despite her natural advantages, however, Moll learns that she lacks one thing that would make her sought after in marriage by gentlemen. She learns that charm, wit, grace and beauty are insufficient assets to the gentle world if money is missing. She overhears a conversation between one of the daughters and the younger son in the family:

> 'I wonder at you, brother,' says the sister; 'Betty [Moll] wants but one thing, but she had as good want every thing, for the market is against our sex just now; and if the young woman has beauty, birth, breeding, wit, sense, manners, modesty, and all these to an extreme, yet if she have not money, she's no body, she had as good want them all; nothing but money now recommends a woman; the men play the game all into their own hand.'

So the scene is set for mercantile principles to infect young Moll. It is worth noting, in this context, Defoe's ironical use of point of view in narration. Moll recollects that the young gentle-women 'were as heartily willing to learn me everything that they had been taught themselves, as I could be to take the learning'. Moll, either as the young woman concerned or as the old woman recounting her memories, sees nothing ironic in this, but Defoe's handling of the matter leaves us in no doubt that Moll's values are corrupted by her supposed superiors and benefactors.

The elder brother of the family makes amorous advances. Moll, flustered and pleased, encourages him. Unlike Richardson's Pamela, she does not hold out for marriage. Her vanity, combined with her attraction to gentility and the wealth which underpins it, results in her fall from virtue. She is consumed with the pride of 'being loved by such a gentleman' as the elder brother, who is always putting 'a handful of gold' in her hand while gratifying her vanity by flattering references to her beauty. The pattern of flattery and reward which, as we have seen, was instrumental in Moll's determination as a young girl to stick to her aim of becoming a gentlewoman, is repeated significantly (and ominously) as Defoe charts her capitulation to the advances of the elder son. He fires her blood, it is true; but she is not unaware of the pleasing possibility of becoming a lady by marriage to one who is destined to inherit the family estate; and she appreciates the desirability of money in furthering her social ambitions: 'As for the gold, I spent whole hours in looking upon it; I told the guineas over a thousand

times a day.' It is perhaps possible to give Moll the benefit of the
doubt and argue[1] that the coins represent the addenda rather than
the principia of the love-making, but it is significant (and again
ominously so) that as the elder brother's passions mount, the sum
of money he gives to Moll seems to rise proportionately: '. . . says
he, here's an earnest for you; and with that he pulls out a silk purse
with an hundred guineas in it, and gave it me . . .'. Defoe's ironic
use of the word 'earnest' can scarcely be doubted, especially since
at the beginning of this episode Moll the narrator had told us that
the whole trouble was that she 'was in earnest, and the gentleman
was not'. Her 'earnest' meant a desire for a genuine and secure
human relationship leading to marriage. The gentleman's 'earnest'
is a silk purse with a hundred guineas in it. Moll is in love with
him; but she is also in love with the idea of becoming the wife of
such a gentleman. Ironically, therefore, her desire to become a
gentlewoman plays its part in her becoming a whore.

When the elder brother refuses to marry her, she decides—dis-
illusioned but determined to make the social grade—to marry
Robin, the younger brother who loves her. The elder, knowing
Moll's social aspirations, advises her to accept the younger's
offer, because in this way she will be able to 'marry a gentleman of
good family, in good circumstances' after all. He seeks to mitigate
the blow by giving her £500 for the liberties which he has taken
with her person—a calculable offence, apparently. Moll takes both
the advice and the money, offering the extenuating plea that she is
'terrified' at the idea of 'being turned out to the wide world a mere
cast-off whore'. She is also influenced in her decision by 'the easy,
prosperous life' she will have as the wife of Robin, 'who, by the
way, I had not the least affection for'. So she finds herself a gentlewoman by loveless marriage.

When Robin's death leaves her a widow with about £1,200, she
has become a changed woman: 'Being still young and handsome . . .
and with a tolerable fortune in my pocket,' she observes, 'I put no
small value upon myself.' By now she has become a social snob.
She is courted by several tradesmen and, though she declares that
she is 'not adverse to a tradesman' (the negative nature of the
assertion is in itself a measure of her increased sophistication), she

---

[1] As does Robert Columbus in his stimulating paper 'Conscious Artistry in
Moll Flanders', *Studies in English Literature*, Vol. III (1963), p. 421.

insists on having a tradesman who 'was something of a gentleman too'. She finally marries a showy 'gentleman-tradesman' whose trade is that of a draper but who has pretensions 'to look like quality'. But the ostentatiously extravagant way of life which they cultivate leads inevitably to their financial ruin. They ride around in 'a rich coach', with an expensive entourage of liveried atten-dants: 'a coachman, postillion, and two footmen . . . a gentleman on horseback, and a page with a feather in his hat . . .' At Oxford they instruct the servants to address them as 'my lord' and 'Countess'. Predictably, in little over two years, they have to flee to the refuge of the Mint.

It is unnecessary to trace in detail Moll's subsequent career. It is sufficient to point out that her formative education in gentility has a lasting effect on her and provides the story with a continuous thread of interest. Her intermittent periods of paralysing fear on the loss of the security of a husband or paramour (i.e. provider) are consistently presented in relation to her true aim in life: 'I knew what I aimed at, and what I wanted . . . I wanted to be placed in a settled state of living.' This candid admission by Moll is the key to understanding both her and her career but it is an admission that is characteristically not susceptible of simple interpretation. Its apparent simplicity is complicated by the fact that a settled state for her means to be able to live like a gentlewoman. So when she seeks to absolve herself of all moral responsibility for her actions by saying that 'vice came in always at the door of necessity, not at the door of inclination', we must be careful to understand her use of the word 'necessity'. Like her creator, she seems to have a unique interpretation of that term. Defoe's apparently sympathetic atti-tude towards Moll's motivation would seem to be the confirmation of what he had written earlier in the *Review*:

> Men rob for bread, women whore for bread; necessity is the parent of crime. Ask the worst highwayman in the nation, ask the lewdest strumpet in the town, if they would not willingly leave off the trade if they could live handsomely without it, and I dare say not one but will acknowledge it.[1]

Defoe appears to be writing about 'necessity', but in fact the opera-

[1] *Review* (VIII, 303).

tive word in the passage is 'handsomely'. Clearly men would not steal and women whore if they had the means to live 'handsomely' without recourse to such devices. This was precisely the kind of moral relativism favoured by Becky Sharp. She, like Moll, schemes only to secure the kind of genteel way of life that 'five thousand a year' could provide. Just that.

Moll does not conceal her compelling desire to live like a woman of quality. When she returns from her prosperous *modus vivendi* in the colonies, she is drawn instinctively to Bath, the favourite resort of people of quality. She takes a maid, hires a coach, dresses expensively and, as the mistress of 'a complete gentleman', is given enough money 'to subsist on very hand-somely'. She is, to a considerable extent, the product of her early shaping environment. She must live 'handsomely', otherwise she feels she is not living at all. Style matters even more than security, though they are obviously related. That is why the social aspect of the story is even more important than the economic, though it is the latter that has evoked most discussion by critics. Her marriage to James, her Lancashire husband, is a direct result of her inability to resist the outward symbols and trappings of gentility.

It is important, likewise, to distinguish the motives which subsequently lead her to embark on a life of crime. When she begins her criminal career, Defoe presents her as driven to it by necessity. Friendless, and low in funds, she is 'driven by the dreadful necessity of [her] circumstances', both physical and psychological. Her entry into crime is mitigated, if not entirely justified, by the Biblical injunction, 'Give me not poverty lest I steal'. Defoe is sympathetic up to a point (as, to judge from his own career, he had good reason to be), but he is later quite explicit in condemning her for continuing to thieve when she has a chance to give up crime and refuses:

> ... the temptation of necessity, which is the general introduc-tion of all such wickedness, was now removed; that I had near £500 by me in ready money, on which I might have lived very well, if I had thought fit to have retired; but I say, I had not so much as the least inclination to leave off.

Moll is now guilty by her own admission and must atone for her crimes. There is a grimly ironic touch of poetic justice in being apprehended by a constable for stealing and locked up in Newgate prison, the very place where she had been born some sixty years previously. Her life has come full circle.

Newgate represents the nadir of Moll's fortunes. But with the assistance of a minister she becomes 'a true penitent', and just as her mother had repented of her life of crime and later prospered in Virginia, so Moll repents of her past life as whore and thief and begins a new way of life in the colonies. Like mother, like daughter. The story has a neat symmetry. The colonial theme, which so attracted Defoe, is his means of restoring Moll to her status as a gentlewoman.[1] Always alert in the overall control of his material, he has prepared us for this by the remark of Moll's mother at the time of her first trip to the colonies: 'many a Newgate-bird becomes a great man' in America. The connection is made when Moll sums up her fate: 'in a word, I was become a mere Newgate-bird'. Defoe is nothing if not a conscious artist.

There is a pleasing irony, as well as continuity of theme, in the fact that colonial wealth gives Moll the opportunity to make James and herself the affluent people of quality they both pretended to be when they deceived each other into marriage many years earlier. Virginia Woolf aptly observed[2] how true it is to Moll's obsession with the idea of a gentleman that she should show such pleasure in attending to her husband's gentlemanly needs:

> I took especial care to buy for him all those things that I knew he delighted to have; as two good long wigs, two silver-hilted swords, three or four fowling-pieces, a fine saddle with holsters and pistols very handsome, with a scarlet cloak; and in a word, everything I could think of to oblige him, and to make him appear, as he really was, a very fine gentleman.

Thus, by his skilful control of the theme of middle-class gentility, Defoe can provide a neat conclusion to his novel by giving Moll the status of gentlewoman, to which she had aspired since early childhood. The child, if we may adapt Wordsworth to the occasion, is mother of the woman, even if their days can scarcely be said to be 'bound each to each by natural piety'.

[1] Michael Shinagel notes this in his valuable study, *Daniel Defoe and Middle-Class Gentility* (Harvard U.P. 1968), p. 159.
[2] Virginia Woolf: 'Defoe' (1919), *The Common Reader* (New York 1948), p. 130.

Piety, or rather the lack of it, brings us, finally, to what was earlier called the logic of spiritual change in *Moll Flanders*. Defoe has a soul to unriddle as well as a career to expound. The coherence with which he organizes his material on this level complements that which he achieves on the other. It is this dual success, each intimately related to the other, that gives the book a deeper unity than has commonly been recognized. On the level of mere plot, Moll's is a success story. In worldly, material terms, she gains her ends. But she comes perilously near to losing her own soul in the process, and the prosperity in which her memoirs end is no guarantee that her repentance is complete, though it seems to be presented as some kind of bulwark to the moral life. Success, which tends, except in the finest characters, to vulgarize all that it touches, is not easily attained without some degree of spiritual compromise. Below the surface level of Moll's story, relating it to a standard of values not of this world, is the record of sin and its consequences for the individual soul. Every rise in society is accompanied by serious moral compromise, that area of life in which the Devil has *his* most subtle and damaging successes. He is usually content that his victims will have the appearance of success as long as he has the reality of their actual failure. Even when Moll is seeing her earlier self from the supposed vantage point of a converted sinner, she tends at times to show something of the Devil's own ingenuity in masking delinquency behind a confusing complexity of motivations, excuses and external pressures. What is excluded or played down in her narrative is often at least as significant as what is included or emphasized.

Take the seduction scene, for example, which is perhaps the decisive initial action on both the social and the spiritual level. All sorts of extenuating factors and circumstances are adduced, which have the effect of clouding our judgement with the specious pleas of moral relativism. First, of course, there is a degree of apparent candour calculated to forestall criticism. Then there is the negative approach that presents misconduct as being at least not calculated, merely foolish. Allied to these tactics in sympathetic presentation is the subtle insinuation that most, if not all, of the initiative came from the man. To passivity, moreover, is added the suggestion of ingenuousness ('as if there was no such things as any kind of love but that which tended to matrimony'). If the reader were to respond uncritically to this surface complexity of motives and pressures, the cumulative effect of these touches would be to minimize the element of deliberate choice on Moll's part. Here is a poor lass deluded by promises and ensnared by the wiles of a practised seducer. All these details are part of a softening-up process designed to enforce a distinction between an act and its circumstances. In this particular case we are being gently but unmistakably pressurized to see a seduction in the total context of the various factors that complicate its moral status. It is presented very skilfully, and indeed in a way that may commend itself to the permissive ideas of our own day. But if a susceptible modern reader is apt to lose his moral bearings in the process, it will be because he is responding to only one level of presentation. Defoe does indeed take into account the external forces that contribute to Moll's seduction; but these forces do not lessen her own responsibility for the deed.

Vanity, as much as anything, is a contributory factor in her undoing. From the age of eight Moll, as we have seen, aspires to be a gentlewoman. The desire itself may be innocent enough but it becomes increasingly an obsession. Moreover, from the time she is ten she is accustomed to hearing herself described as 'pretty', and she confesses that this made her 'not a little proud'. Defoe is careful to indicate that it is vanity rather than love or lust which motivates her conduct at the beginning of her relationship with the elder brother. She does indeed become passionately attached to him in the course of time, but initially this is not present as the chief animating factor in her seduction. When his declarations of love 'fire her blood' we must not at this stage impart a Laurentian flavour to the phrase, for Defoe makes it clear that it is her vanity which is inflamed. Thus Moll reports that

> my head ran upon strange things, and I may truly say I was not myself, to have such a gentleman talk to me of being in love with me, and of my being such a charming creature, as he told me I was. These things I knew not how to bear; my vanity was elevated to the last degree.

So, too, when the courtship is well under way, she makes the significant distinction that 'This gentleman had now fired his inclination as much as he had my vanity'. Later Moll states emphatically that 'that which I was too vain of was my ruin, or rather my vanity was the cause of it'; and she describes herself as 'a fair memento to all young women whose vanity prevails over their virtue'. By furnishing the elder brother with an abundance of guile and gold, and by placing Moll in what amounts to the situation of a chambermaid,[1] Defoe is duly taking into consideration the context of a given act, but I cannot see that in the process he is calling in question the notion that an act is inherently right or wrong. In fact, far from lessening her own responsibility for moral choice, these external forces scarcely even, in the last resort, complicate that choice but rather give impetus to the vanity which chiefly determines her behaviour.

Between her seduction and her conversion, a process of hardening forms the basic pattern of Moll's spiritual development. The process gives a certain continuity to her behaviour. Her vanity, for instance, seems to be strangely insulated against the mortification which she might be expected to feel on noting the increasing lack of ceremony with which the elder brother treats her. The lack of love—lust in action—shows itself in his increasing tendency simply to use her as a means of personal gratification. There is a horrible disparity between the love which she professes to feel for the man and the plainness with which she describes her relations with him:

... tired with that kind of work ...
... he comes up again in about half an hour, and falls to work with me again just as he did before, only with a little less introduction ...
When this was over he stayed but a little while ...
... if he had known me and how easy the trifle he aimed at was to be had, he would have troubled his head no farther, but have given me four or five guineas and have lain with me the next time he had come at me.

The relationship is recorded with about as much feeling and delicacy as one might expect in the language of a stud-book.

The process of disintegration is at once caused and revealed by the attempt to anaesthetize her emotions. From ignoring her feelings

[1] See M. Novak: *Economics and the Fiction of Daniel Defoe* (Berkeley 1962), pp. 84–85.

(by entering into a loveless marriage with Robin for the sake of social status and security) to being incapable of sympathy or fellow-feeling with the child whom she robs (and who is called 'it') is but a short step. The tragic swiftness of disintegration, the loss of the 'single state of man', is told in *Macbeth*. Moll, of course, lacks the potential greatness necessary for tragedy, but the collapse of integrity shows itself in many instances where she lacks the capacity for a feeling for others strong enough to survive conflict with her own interest. Her unwillingness to have abortions is human enough, certainly, by today's standards, but it has to be said that maternal feeling never prevents her from eventually disposing of her children when they become inconvenient to her; and whatever injury is done to that maternal feeling by the separation seems always to heal quite soon. Only two of Moll's attachments endure, her relationships with the governess and with Jemmy, her Lancashire husband.

Her protestations of moral sentiment are no less specious. Her account of robbing the child mentioned above is accompanied by a homily on the vanity of parents; and after she has given herself to a drunken 'gentleman' in exchange for the opportunity to rifle his pockets, she proceeds to inveigh against the sins of drunkenness and lechery. It is true that Moll is first moved to steal out of 'necessity'. Her initial theft is extenuated by the plea that there 'are temptations which it is not in the power of human nature to resist'.[1] But in the same sentence she notes that 'as covetousness is the root of all evil, so poverty is the worst of all snares'. Thus the plea of poverty opens a breach for covetousness. Necessity swells, inflated by avarice. What is at one point in her life necessity gradually becomes inclination. Self-command yields to desire and circumstance, and in the process moral discrimination and judgement are first impaired and then lost. As she observed of an earlier lapse, with the Bath lover, 'the way being thus cleared, and the bars of virtue and conscience thus removed, we had the less to struggle with'. Necessity may extenuate an initial lapse but if repentance does not follow, the lapse becomes a settled course of action. Outwardly, Moll's is a success story: inwardly it is an imaginative demonstration of the way in which sin leads to more

[1] Cf. M. Novak's article on 'The Problem of Necessity in Defoe's Fiction', *PQ* XL (1961) 513–24.

sin, and of how evil can diminish the freedom to do good. Hardened by success, her will has become enslaved.

One could trace the continuation of this process in greater detail, but we may turn now, finally, to the scene of her imprisonment in Newgate. This 'emblem of hell' has been regarded as a powerful indictment of contemporary prison conditions, which had the effect of more often hardening criminals than reclaiming them. Defoe's portrayal of the Newgate Ordinary, preaching confession and repentance in the morning, dead drunk with brandy by noon, is part of a forcible expression of reforming indignation. Yet his quite justifiable concern, here as elsewhere, with the powerful influences of environment does not preclude a fundamental concern with the spiritual condition of Moll. Society may be responsible, to a considerable extent, for her outward vicissitudes, but basically it is her own reactions to them that give rise to her spiritual predicament.

When Moll does finally repent, the genuineness of her state (however temporary) can be gauged, as Professor Starr has pointed out, not only by its contrast with all the abortive versions that have preceded it, but also by its conformity to the classic pattern of spiritual rebirth. Her reawakening out of utter 'lethargy of soul' makes her more susceptible to the exhortations of the minister who visits her after her trial. She reviews her past life and laments her sins not merely from fear of human punishment, but with a consciousness of having offended against God and man, and with a concern for the state of her immortal soul:

> It was now that, for the first time, I felt any real signs of repentance. I now began to look back upon my past life with abhorrence, and having a kind of view into the other side of time, the things of life ... began to look with a different aspect, and quite another shape, than they did before.

All of Defoe's stories are, as Bonamy Dobrée observes,[1] 'success stories', but with this important qualification: 'his heroes and heroines all make good, indeed reach affluence, in the end, after tottering at the edge of the abyss'. Once their quest for status and security is achieved, safe from the temptations of 'necessity', they

[1] Bonamy Dobrée: *English Literature in the Early Eighteenth Century* (Oxford 1964), p. 415.

are free to address themselves to higher matters and repent. In *Moll Flanders* he has written a story of sin and its consequences as well as of a woman's rise to material success. We have the external story of Moll's career, of how she eventually achieves her life-long ambition to become a gentlewoman; and most of what are often dismissed by critics as mere 'episodes' are in fact related to this theme. We have also the inward, spiritual story, the fable of what happened to Moll in the process of 'making good'. Each is coherent, the one providing its gloss on the other. The unity of the book is rooted in the tensions between the social and economic aspirations of the protagonist and her moral or religious scruples, the difficulties of being good in the process of 'making good'. *Experto crede.* It was an aspect of life of which Defoe had first-hand experience. In this novel, as in others, he seeks, to some extent, to harmonize the conflicts between the one way of life and the other through the theme of repentance. But it is an uneasy harmony at best. Moll Flanders repents but keeps her ill-gotten gains. God and Mammon are not thus easily reconciled.

The implication of the story would seem to be that if repentance is to outlast the immediate fears that so largely (though not exclusively) induced it, the penitent must have some degree of financial and social security. In his *Serious Reflections during the Life and Surprising Adventures of Robinson Crusoe* Defoe expressed the view that 'Necessity is above the power of human nature, and for Providence to suffer a man to fall into that necessity is to suffer him to sin, because nature is not furnished with power to defend itself, nor grace to fortify the mind against it'.[1] The trouble is that Moll's motive in amassing so much of her money and goods had not been to mitigate the pressures of downright 'necessity' but to satisfy ruthless ambitions. The outward story of how she had 'acquired' the money and possessions is a fascinating story of brains, beauty, enterprise and courage in pursuit of a goal. But the moral fable, as we have seen, makes clear that vanity and greed, not 'necessity', came to determine her use of these qualities. Inevitably, therefore, the reader's attitude to the sincerity, or rather completeness, of Moll's repentance in relation to keeping the fruits of her criminal life must be affected by an awareness of this distinction. If Defoe's silence on this distinction seems to argue a

[1] *Romances and Narrative by Daniel Defoe,* ed. Aitken (London 1895), Vol. III, p. 35.

degree of moral ambiguity at odds with some of the high-minded authorial professions in the Preface, it is no doubt a reflection of the ambiguity inherent in the mercantile society of his day; and it does not impair the unity of a novel which from first to last has been concerned with the difficulties of reconciling social aspirations and the life of the spirit.

BIBLIOGRAPHY

Texts

DEFOE, DANIEL: *Moll Flanders*

Modern Library College edition (New York 1950) contains stimulating Introduction by Mark Schorer.

World's Classics edition (Oxford U.P. 1961), a modernized reprinting of the first edition, which was published in 1722.

Fawcett paperback edition (1967) contains a valuable 'Afterword' by Ian Watt. This essay appeared originally as 'The Recent Critical Fortunes of *Moll Flanders*' in *Eighteenth-Century Studies* I (1967) 109–26.

Oxford English Novels edition, ed. G. A. Starr (Oxford U.P., London 1971) is very helpful.

Critical Works

(a) Articles on *Moll Flanders* in Periodicals:

Brooks, Douglas: '*Moll Flanders;* An Interpretation', *ECr* XIX (1969) 46–59.

Columbus, Robert R.: 'Conscious Artistry in *Moll Flanders*', *Studies in English Literature* III (1963) 415–32.

Donoghue, Denis: 'The Values of *Moll Flanders*', *Sewanee Review* LXXI (1963) 287–303.

Koonce, Howard: 'Moll's Muddle: Defoe's Use of Irony in *Moll Flanders*', *Journal of English Literary History* XXX (1963) 377–94.

Martin, Terence: 'The Unity of *Moll Flanders*', *MLQ* XXII (1961) 115–24.

(b) Books containing discussions of *Moll Flanders*:

Alter, Robert: *Rogue's Progress: Studies in the Picaresque Novel* (Cambridge, Mass. 1964).

Butt, John (ed.): *Of Books and Humankind: Essays and Poems Presented to Bonamy Dobrée* (London 1964) contains chapter 'In Defence of *Moll Flanders*' by Arnold Kettle.

Dobrée, Bonamy: *English Literature in the Early Eighteenth Century, 1700–1740* (Oxford 1959).

Donovan, Robert A.: *The Shaping Vision* (New York 1966).

Elliott, Robert C. (ed.): *Twentieth-Century Interpretations of Moll Flanders* (Englewood Cliffs, N.J. 1970 [Spectrum Books]).

Lonsdale, Roger (ed.): *Sphere History of Literature in the English Language, Dryden to Johnson* (London 1971) contains a chapter on 'Defoe and Richardson' by Mark Kinkead-Weekes.

McKillop, A. D.: *The Early Masters of English Fiction* (Lawrence, Kansas 1956; London 1962).

Novak, Maximilian: *Economics and the Fiction of Daniel Defoe* (Berkeley 1962); and *Defoe and the Nature of Man* (London 1963).

Parker, Alexander A.: *Literature and the Delinquent* (Edinburgh 1967).

Price, Martin: *To the Palace of Wisdom* (Southern Illinois U.P. 1964).

Shinagel, Michael: *Daniel Defoe and Middle-Class Gentility* (Cambridge, Mass. 1968).

Starr, George A.: *Defoe and Spiritual Biography* (Princeton 1965); and *Defoe and Casuistry* (Princeton 1971).

Sutherland, James: *Defoe* (London 1937; 2nd edition 1950); and *Daniel Defoe; A Critical Study* (Cambridge, Mass. 1971).

Van Ghent, Dorothy: *The English Novel: Form and Function* (New York 1953).

Watt, Ian: *The Rise of the Novel* (London 1957).

A. R. STRUGNELL

Diderot's *Neveu de Rameau*: Portrait of a Rogue in the French Enlightenment

H OW CAN ONE JUSTIFY THE INCLUSION OF THIS STRANGE
and remarkable work in a symposium on the European
picaresque novel? To begin with it can hardly be called a novel; the
hybrid term novel-dialogue comes nearer to providing an objective
description of it for the modern reader. Furthermore, although
Diderot must have read some Spanish picaresque novels, if not in
the 'improved' seventeenth-century translations, then at least in
the equally distorted versions of *Guzmán de Alfarache* and *Estevanillo
González* published by Lesage in 1732, there is no clear evidence to
show that he was influenced by them, or by Lesage's own *Gil Blas*
for that matter. In this respect Diderot is typical of French writers
of fiction in the eighteenth century. With the sole exception of
Gil Blas, no novel can in strict literary-historical terms be said to
have been cast in the picaresque mould. *Gil Blas* is the last and
perhaps best example of a series of novels starting with Sorel's
Francion (1622) which clearly owe a debt to the Spanish tradition,
and which constitute the beginnings of realist fiction in France.
Yet numerous critics have apparently felt justified in applying the
term picaresque to later works which, although not strictly belong-
ing to the genre, are nonetheless inheritors of the characteristics
injected into the French literary tradition by it. Thus we find
aspects of Marivaux's *Paysan parvenu*, Restif de la Bretonne's
Monsieur Nicolas, Voltaire's *Candide* and even Rousseau's *Confessions*
labelled as picaresque. This has led to calls for caution on the part

of some critics,[1] alarmed at what they see to be a misuse of a term
which has become increasingly detached from its original function
as the description of a quite specific literary subject and form.

This caution is surely quite justified where the notions of the
picaresque and the *pícaro* are expanded to include Julien Sorel in
Stendhal's *Le Rouge et le Noir*[2] whose refined sensibility, nobility
and pride take him out of the rogue class, or Camus' novels.[3] In the
latter case the concept has been turned on its head in the figure of
the picaresque saint, a meaningless label if ever there was one,
whatever the merit of the literary studies which come under its
heading. Nevertheless, despite these eccentric exaggerations I do
not think that the alternative is necessarily to retreat into a purist
literary-historical position which refuses to see picaresque elements
in any work of fiction, unless the influence has been clearly proven
by substantial affinities of structure, style and theme, as well as
external evidence. This attitude is particularly unhelpful in the
field of eighteenth-century French fiction, where the picaresque
tradition was willy-nilly an element in the literary awareness of
contemporary writers, whether or not it can be shown conclusively
that they were influenced by it. Thus it is unduly severe to maintain, as does Vivienne Mylne, that it is not 'either relevant or useful
to compare (Jacob) with Gil Blas or to call the *Paysan parvenu* a
"picaresque" novel',[4] since Jacob has much in common with the
picaresque anti-hero as modified by Lesage. Admittedly he differs
from Gil Blas in that his social climb is largely through his success
with women, but like Lesage's hero he reaches the top by using his
native talents, taking advantage of good fortune and learning from
his mistakes. Both novels are picaresque in that they describe in
episodic fashion the adventures of a socially mobile protagonist of
modest origins within the framework of a varied and picturesque
social reality. *Le Paysan parvenu* is, as Frédéric Deloffre has shown,[5]
not distinct from the French picaresque genre as represented by
Lesage, but an enrichment of it.

[1] See W. M. Frohock: 'The Idea of the Picaresque', in *Yearbook of Comparative and General Literature* XVI (1967) 43–52.
[2] See R. Alter: *Rogue's Progress: Studies in the Picaresque Novel* (Cambridge, Mass. 1964), pp. 109–13.
[3] See R. W. B. Lewis: *The Picaresque Saint* (London 1960), pp. 57–108.
[4] *The Eighteenth-Century Novel* (Manchester U.P. 1965), p. 122.
[5] In the introduction to his edition of *Le Paysan parvenu* (Paris 1965).

The essential point to be borne in mind, as Philippe van Tieghem has indicated,[1] is that the very realism which forms the essence of the picaresque novel excludes a direct and literal influence, which would be the very negation of realism, inasmuch as the latter consists of observing real life and not utilizing a literary theme. Consequently, while *Gil Blas* is not the tale of a shameless and cynical swindler from a morally sordid background like the *pícaro* Guzmán, it is nonetheless a novel within the picaresque tradition, adapted by Lesage to the portrayal of the social reality of Regency France. Similarly it can be argued that *Le Paysan parvenu* is a further adaptation, this time of the Lesagian picaresque, required by the introduction of a psychological reality which is not prominent in *Gil Blas*. The reason why Lesage and Marivaux could write novels which bear a marked similarity with the Spanish originals is that the social reality which they sought to convey in them had much in common with the setting in which the Spanish *pícaros* lived out their adventures. Both French and Spanish novels can be seen to portray feudal society at critical stages in its disintegration. But whereas in the Spanish novel the perspective is bleakly pessimistic since there is nothing to replace the decaying feudalism of agrarian seventeenth-century Spain, in the French novel of the beginning of the eighteenth century the outlook is essentially optimistic, for the portrayal of feudal decadence is set within the perspective of the ascension of the bourgeois in the persons of Gil Blas and Jacob.[2] It can therefore be seen that the picaresque form and the picaresque hero provided a malleable literary convention within which the emergent conflict between middle-class and feudal values in eighteenth-century France could be posed in artistic terms.

As the century progressed social and political circumstances changed. By the mid-century the incipient anarchy of the Regency was little more than a bad memory, the monarchy having re-established and consolidated its firm centralizing grip over the nation. But at the same time the bourgeoisie had emerged as a militant cultural and ideological force, increasingly hostile to the orthodox values of the Church and Parlements, to which it opposed

[1] *Les Influences étrangères sur la littérature française (1550–1880)* (Paris 1961), p. 43.
[2] See Werner Bahner: 'Quelques Observations sur le genre picaresque', in *Roman et lumières au XVIIIe siècle* (Paris 1970) 71–72.

its own moral code raised to the status of an ideal. The climate was no longer suited to the writing of novels in the style of *Gil Blas* whose parvenu heroes represented an earlier bourgeois morality of adaptation to an aristocratic ethos. But while the picaresque form as such was not an appropriate vehicle for the depiction of the now open conflict of the two cultures, various elements of the genre persisted in dispersal in the literary production of the latter half of the century, notably the journeying hero of modest origins or of delinquent behaviour, and the portrayal of a cross-section of society. Writers of libertine, philosophical and autobiographical novels consciously or unconsciously dipped into the picaresque tradition. For a society that was intensely curious about itself and increasingly fascinated with the problem of the individual's relationship to the collectivity the picaresque, which had been the first genre capable of accommodating this form of enquiry, still had something to offer.

It is within this socio-literary context that *Le Neveu de Rameau* was written, a novel dialogue whose rogue-hero is a spiritual descendant of the Spanish *pícaros* who were first responsible for the establishment of the anti-social delinquent or at least the amoral rascal as an accepted literary figure in France. As a rogue Rameau in his behaviour and attitude to life has more in common with Spanish *pícaros* such as Lazarillo and Guzmán than does Gil Blas, whose misfortunes are temporary and whose immorality is redeemable. He, like them, spends most of his time and energy warding off the pangs of hunger and ensuring he has a bed for the night. He is a genuine down-and-out of fairly modest origins—his father was an apothecary—who is forced to live off his wits and for whom the virtuous morality of the Philosopher, his interlocutor, is a luxury he could not afford even if he wanted to. In his eyes, society is governed by an unyieldingly cruel law of nature by which all classes prey upon one another just as the animal species do. The idea of selfless duty towards family, friends and community is a pathetic vanity. The only sensible aim in life is to get to the top of the pile as quickly as possible and by whatever means, and it is in the nature of things that base flattery, lying, cheating and deceit are the surest keys to success. Rameau prides himself on being a past master in all these arts, and a pimp and procurer into the bargain. His sole ambition, if ever he can hoist himself out of his present wretched condition is, as he tells Moi,[1] to 'drink good wine, blow yourself out with luscious food, have a tumble with lovely women, lie on soft beds' (p. 65). Rameau also has the *pícaro's* experience of all manners and conditions of men and, as Deloffre has noted,[2] the verve with which he recounts his adventures is strongly reminiscent of the picaresque narrative. His encounters are legion and range widely over the social spectrum: he has sat at the table of a minister of the King, been resident clown in the household of the financier Bertin, lured innocent young shopgirls into the arms of rich young aristocrats, pimped his wife around Paris, taught music to the children of the wealthy, begged a bed in the straw from a coachman, travelled around Europe as a servant to a Jew, and so on. The list is a long one. In common with the Spanish *pícaros* Rameau has a worm's-eye view of the world; everyone he meets is either his social equal or superior. Like them too he constantly uses irony to emphasize the gulf between the values those above him claim to live by and those which in fact determine their behaviour. But given these similarities, which may lead us to speculate that there may be an as yet undiscovered literary-historical link between *Le Neveu* and the Spanish *pícaro,* Rameau is also a remarkable example of the adaptability of the rogue-figure in European literature. As a rogue he is unmistakably a child of his own age and culture and is used by Diderot to reflect and criticize some of the fundamental issues of the Enlightenment.

Le Neveu de Rameau takes the form of a desultory conversation between Moi, the narrator, a philosopher by calling, and Lui, the nephew of the famous composer, Rameau, and himself a musician and would-be composer. Their meeting takes place at the Régence, a famous coffee-house still in existence and then a favourite venue for Parisian chess players. The Philosopher has taken refuge there from the inclement weather that has driven him away from the gardens of the Palais-Royal where he is in the habit of spending the early evening in solitary meditation. While, in his apparently habitual role of observer, watching the chess players make their

---

[1] All quotations from *Le Neveu* are taken from *Rameau's Nephew and D'Alembert's Dream,* trans. L. W. Tancock (Harmondsworth 1966) and page numbers following quotations refer to this version. I have, however, preferred the French pronominal designations of the characters, Moi and Lui, to those of the translation, I and He.

[2] Op. cit., p. vii.

moves, he is accosted by Rameau who forces him out of his passive
role and involves him in prolonged conversation on topics as
diverse as Rameau's experiences in the households of the rich, the
nature of genius, the superiority of Italian music over French, the
contemporary literary scene, education, and Rameau's failure to
achieve material success in life. All of these subjects are woven into
a wider discussion on morality and art. This anarchic profusion of
themes, apparently linked by nothing more than the association of
ideas common to conversations arising out of a chance meeting,
imbues the work with a spontaneity and realism unique to French
literature of the time. However, beneath the semblance of disorder
there lies a subtle and complex structure. It has been compared
with the form of a musical composition which 'progresses by relations, that is, by oblique and affinitive communication',[1] and with
a line passing diametrically through series of concentric circles,
each series representing a group of subjects, so that each subject is
touched on twice, thus conferring on the successive sections of the
dialogue a certain symmetry.[2] A further analogy can be made with
a game of chess, thus attributing to the opening paragraphs a
symbolic significance, and indeed it is the conflictual aspect of
Le Neveu de Rameau which has particularly preoccupied commen-
tators, and which has led to the greatest divergence of opinion as
to the work's significance. There are those who hold that at the
end of the dialogue Rameau has won the trial of moral and intellectual strength with the Philosopher, thereby vindicating creative
human individuality solidly couched in the realities of this world
in the face of a sterile and dogmatising moralism complacently
aloof from the affairs of men.[3] On the other hand there are those,
in the majority, who award the victory to Moi, whose modesty,
moral integrity and artistic fertility stand out forcefully against the
moral corruption and artistic mediocrity of Lui.[4] I suppose it is

[1] Jean-Pierre Baricelli: 'Music and the Structure of Diderot's *Le Neveu de Rameau*',
Criticism V (1963) 98.
[2] James Doolittle: *Rameau's Nephew* (Paris-Geneva 1960), p. 21.
[3] This is essentially the view of Doolittle, op. cit., Roger Laufer in his chapter on
Le Neveu de Rameau in his *Style Rococo, style des lumières* (Paris 1963) and R. Grimsley,
in 'Psychological Aspects of *Le Neveu de Rameau*', *MLQ* XVI (1955) 195–209.
[4] The most recent adherents to this view are M. Duchet, in *Entretiens sur 'Le
Neveu de Rameau'* (Paris 1967), M. Launay, ibid., p. 233, R. Desné, ibid., p. 507
and N. L. Sandomirsky in 'The Ethical Standard of the Genius in Diderot's
Neveu de Rameau', *Symposium* XVIII (1964) 46–55.

impossible to discuss the book without taking sides in the debate, but my intention is not so much to do this as to show how Diderot draws from the conflict which Rameau provokes with his interlocutor a new understanding of the moral life, and presents in his portrayal of a rogue an apology for the uniqueness and irreducibility of human individuality.

Rameau is not a straightforward rogue, nor are his adventures simply an excuse for Diderot to paint a realistic canvas of the seamier sides of Parisian society in the latter half of the eighteenth century. In terms of perspective *Le Neveu de Rameau* is quite different from the autobiographical picaresque novel, where it is the *pícaro* who provides the angle of vision from which the reader views his character and exploits. In *Le Neveu* the perspective is determined not by Lui but by Moi, whose observations on Rameau in a passage from the opening pages of the book are of key importance for our understanding of the text:

> I don't think much of the queer birds myself, though some people make boon companions of them, and even friends. They interest me once a year when I run into them because their characters contrast sharply with other people's and break the tedious uniformity that our social conventions and set politenesses have brought about. If one of them appears in a company of people he is the speck of yeast that leavens the whole and restores to each of us a portion of his natural individuality. He stirs people up and gives them a shaking, makes them take sides, brings out the truth, shows who are really good and unmasks the villains. It is then that the wise man listens and sorts people out. (p. 35)

Rameau's function is to cast off the dissembling mask which society forces upon men, to reveal the natural man hidden beneath the social man, to distinguish between the man of virtue and the scoundrel. His lucidity, impertinence and sincerity are the three qualities which suit him admirably for this role. He has a unique capacity for smelling out cant, hypocrisy and empty posturing wherever they may be found. Openly critical of his own shortcomings, he does not spare others the barbs of his destructively insolent wit. He has no illusions about the motley crowd of artistic and intellectual mediocrities who make up the Bertin-Hus salon from which he has so recently been ejected, and who pass their time in envious denigration of the great and the successful: 'We look jovial, but in reality we are all foul-tempered and voracious of appetite. Wolves are not more famished, tigers no more cruel. We devour like wolves when the earth has been long under snow, like tigers we tear to pieces anything successful.' (p. 80) Bertin himself is gloomy, inscrutable and bordering on the inarticulate, his consort an ignorant and stupid wench, a third-rate actress running to fat, who prides herself on her wit, intelligence and histrionic talents. Behind the façade of elegant repartee and cultivated discussion of the Parisian artistic scene spreads a wasteland of malevolence and sterility.

Diderot, it might be thought, is using Rameau to get even with his enemies. The wily Moi, it could be argued, exploits Lui's impertinent verbosity by carefully placed feeds in order to provide him with the opportunity for entering into a highly amusing and mischievous send-up of the anti-philosophic clan. But such an interpretation, which would reduce *Le Neveu de Rameau* to a cheap caricaturing satire, rests upon two serious misconceptions, the first being that Diderot the author and Moi the narrator and opponent of Lui are to be identified, the second that Rameau's demasking techniques are only effective against the opponents of the *philosophes*. Let it be said straight away that *Le Neveu de Rameau* is not an early essay in documentary hyperrealism. It is true that the references to real events and personalities are legion; Rameau's nephew really did exist and contemporary accounts describe him as an eccentric failed musician, so did Bertin, Hus and Palissot exist, as well as all the other hangers-on. A considerable effort has been made by scholars to identify all the contemporary allusions and it has been shown that Diderot made no effort to change names or confuse identities. But then his creative genius did not seek so much to invent characters and situations as to transform artistically the reality which he experienced in his day-to-day life or which he had heard about at second hand. Thus the real Rameau was only a pale shadow of the monster created by his pen, the Bertin-Hus ménage in reality fell far short of the grotesque mediocrity with which Diderot invests it, and the half-baked real-life Palissot could not have lived up to the role of a great criminal conferred upon him. Similarly Moi is a stylised one-sided version of his creator. In

Le Neveu de Rameau Moi appears as a rather solitary, taciturn figure, slow on the uptake, limited in his awareness of the world around him, inclined to be prudish, and given to dogmatic sermonizing on the merits of the virtuous life. Those characteristics were all in some measure present in the real Diderot, as evidenced by his correspondence and accounts of friends and acquaintances. But they were far from being the only or even the dominant features of his personality, which was more inclined to be exuberantly sociable, open-minded and equipped with a rumbustious and at times scabrous sense of humour. Critics have seized upon different parts of the text to prove both that Moi is Diderot and that he is an invented character quite distinct from his author. The references to Moi's daughter and his stormy relations with his wife are cited to justify the first thesis, the fact that Rameau appears to distinguish between Moi and Diderot as one of the *philosophes* lampooned in Palissot's play of the same name is held to prove the second. In my view Diderot intentionally creates an atmosphere of ambiguity around Moi; he is neither to be wholly identified with him nor distinguished from him. His object thereby is to establish a critical distance between himself as artist and an aspect of his personality which is in disharmony with the rest. This form of literary self-purgation as opposed to the literary self-indulgence practised by Rousseau, rare not to say unique in the French eighteenth century, was to become a fairly common feature of what can be broadly termed autobiographical fiction from the Romantic age onwards. A list of later practitioners could include Stendhal, Goethe, Constant, Chateaubriand, Wilde, Gide and Joyce. In the case of Diderot the purgative, or yeast to use his own image, was Rameau.

Although the perspective of *Le Neveu de Rameau* is ultimately determined by Moi, this does not mean, as has sometimes been suggested, that he always has the upper hand in the conversation with Lui. A closer consideration of the text will show that Rameau's rogue intelligence is at times more than a match for his interlocutor. In the opening part of the dialogue[1] Moi is clearly in control; sure of himself and confident in the values he holds, his manner is calm and condescending towards Lui, who presents a pitiable picture of vicious hatred of the talented and irritable self-reproach for his own

[1] pp. 35–51 of Tancock's translation.

inadequacy. In the discussion on genius Lui ties himself up in a
mass of contradictions which make him easy meat for Moi. At first
he acknowledges that 'in chess, draughts, poetry, eloquence, music
and other nonsense of that kind' only men of genius can be toler-
ated, but he then turns round and dismisses them as anti-social and
the source of all evil, thus judging them by the standards of conventional virtue, which are in turn repudiated by his eulogy of the
parasitic life. In the face of Moi's superior arguments Lui concedes
that the real reason for his loathing of genius is jealousy, and disgust
at his own insufficiency, for he is incapable of achieving greatness
and success in either music or moral turpitude, the two fields in
which he claims distinction. If Rameau loses the debate on genius
it is because he is incapable of raising himself to the level of
abstraction at which it must be pursued. His points of reference are
restricted to his own immediate experience of the world, his needs
and aspirations. However, this weakness becomes a strength when
the drift of the discussion forces Moi off his lofty perch and draws
him down into the world of practical living. When this happens
Lui has an easy time running circles around his opponent, who
flounders hopelessly in a morass of sanctimonious piety and crass
naïvety. Parasites should be denied house-room, procurers should
be beaten, and Rameau's affirmation that scoundrels pride themselves on their vices is received by Moi as something barely
conceivable. And when Rameau proceeds to give a detailed illustration of a vice he has developed to a height of rare perfection by
enacting the scene in which he procures an innocent young girl,
Moi completely loses his composure:

> I was torn between opposite impulses and did not know whether
> to give in to laughter or furious indignation. I felt embarrassed.
> A score of times a burst of laughter prevented a burst of rage,
> and a score of times the anger rising from the depths of my heart
> ended in a burst of laughter. I was dumbfounded at such
> sagacity and such baseness, such alternately true and false
> notions, such absolute perversion of feeling and utter turpitude,
> and yet such uncommon candour. (p. 51)

The first stage in the demasking of the Philosopher has been accomplished; his emotional and philosophical serenity, the fruit of a
rationalistic understanding of the human condition, have not been

able to withstand the furious onslaught of his opponent's defiantly anti-rationalist pragmatism.

Rameau is quick to profit from Moi's dissarray and push his advantage. Attacking him at his weakest points, he reminds Moi that he too had known poverty in his youth, and had been forced to give tuition in mathematics, a subject of which he was woefully ignorant. He points to the folly of his ambition to educate his daughter in worthwhile disciplines rather than the social graces, since success in this world depends on the latter, and besides, her tutors are bound to be incompetent. In the face of Rameau's uncompromising realism Moi's defence of moral rectitude looks distinctly lame. His essential weakness derives from the fact that his inadequate consideration of human affairs in all their rawness and diversity has left a gaping chasm between his philosophical principles and the harsh reality of life being forced in upon his consciousness by the pressing attentions of Lui. But—and this is the telling difference between Moi and Rameau's other 'victims'— embarrassed as he is, he does not, despite every temptation to do so, pull down the shutters of his mind and dismiss the inconvenient Rameau from his presence. His reaction is quite different:

Lui: What are you dreaming about?
Moi: I am reflecting that everything you have said is more specious than logical. But let it go at that. You say you have taught accompaniment and composition? (p. 58)

By changing the subject Moi regains the initiative and diverts Rameau's attention away from himself, but at a more profound level there are signs of a change of attitude; he has become more thoughtful. On several occasions later when Rameau exasperates him he will again react with a mixture of amusement and indignation, but a new mood has begun to overtake him, leading him to adjust his views and modify his philosophy.

This new mood is reflected in the next section of the dialogue[1] in which Moi restricts his interventions to clarificatory questions and remarks. His aim now is not to confute Lui but to observe dispassionately the rascally phenomenon, who has so effectively jolted his most cherished beliefs, by giving him the opportunity to reveal himself in all his degenerate glory. Moi sustains his attitude of

[1] pp. 58–64 of Tancock's translation.

scientific detachment as Rameau regales him with a litany of vice. Flattery and ruse are justified since people in all walks of life use deception in the service of self-advancement. One should feel no compunction about using these means to rob the rich; parasitism and profligacy are two sides of the same coin and a convenient way of restoring the economic balance within society. This unfettered display of cynicism is rounded off with a well-aimed swipe at the main plank of Moi's moral philosophy: 'You think that happiness is the same for all. What a strange illusion! Your own brand presupposes a certain romantic turn of mind that we don't all possess, an unusual type of soul, a peculiar taste. You dignify this oddity with the name of virtue and you call it philosophy. But are virtue and philosophy made for everybody?' (pp. 64–5)

Rameau's sudden reversion to *ad hominem* tactics catches Moi off his guard. He abandons the posture of detached observer and once more rushes into the lists, a Sir Galahad of bourgeois probity lunging at his dastardly enemy with a series of conventional pieties deftly parried by Rameau, who points to their unviability in the world as it is. But this is the last time that Lui will enjoy such an easy victory. The sagacity of many of his remarks has not been lost on Moi, who has begun to realize that doctrinally prescriptive generalizations concerning moral behaviour fail to account for the vast multiplicity of personality and experience. They are only applicable to a non-existent dehumanized stereotype and are bound to disintegrate in the corrosive atmosphere of human realities. Thus it is that in the remaining part of the dialogue Moi's moralizing platitudes and philosophical apophthegms gradually give way to an emphasis on the particular circumstance and the individual case. This approach reveals itself to be far more effective against the attacks of Rameau. In a brief exchange on the idle pleasure-seeking of the fashionable rich it is for once Moi who strikes the more profound note: 'They wear everything out. Their souls run to seed and boredom takes over. In the midst of oppressive opulence it would be a kindness to relieve them of life. All they know of happiness is the part that cloys first' (p. 66). In the self-portrait that follows the pleasure Moi claims to take in living a virtuous life is all the more convincing for being set against an admission that he is not averse to the pleasures of the senses. In this admission Moi has recognized that the very first requirement of the gospel of virtue is that its disciple should not fear to reveal himself in his total humanity, thus bearing witness to the gospel's ability to redeem and fulfil the whole man.

The logical corollary to demonstrating the benefits accruing to those who live according to the gospel of virtue is to prove that contemporary society, which rejects virtue, fails conspicuously in providing the moral environment in which men can live as complete human beings. What better way of doing so than submitting Rameau, who claims in his cultivation of vileness and abjection to be incarnating the 'natural' values on which society rests, to a searching scrutiny? In the rest of the dialogue, seen from the point of view of the Moi-Lui conflict, Moi pursues and finally fulfils his aim of discrediting the *Ancien Régime* through Rameau. When asked, Lui explains that his aim in revealing himself in all his turpitude is to extract from Moi a recognition that he has achieved a degree of greatness in evil which transcends all moral categories: 'It is important to be sublime in anything, it is especially so in evil. You spit on a petty thief, but you can't withhold a sort of respect from a great criminal ... What you value in everything is consistency of character' (p. 93). Later he adds: 'I wanted you to know how I excelled in my art, I wanted to force you to admit that at least I was unique in my degradation, and classify me in your mind with the great blackguards' (p. 96). But Lui is not able to provoke unalloyed admiration, for Moi's feelings are shot through with a 'tinge of ridicule' which discolours them. He knows that Rameau has not achieved the sublimity to which he pretends: 'You haven't got this admirable consistency of character yourself yet. Now and again I catch you vacillating in your principles' (p. 93). Despite every effort to achieve complete self-abasement a remnant of dignity prevents him from practising that total self-commitment which alone can raise human endeavour to the heights of sublimity. The trouble is that he wants to be abject on his own terms, not realizing that true abjectness requires the relinquishment of all rights over oneself, and that even if he were capable of reaching such a state, the spectacle of servile submission would elicit at worst contempt, at best pity, but certainly not the admiration which he craves. In choosing self-abasement as his life-style he is representative of a society which stands condemned, not so much for its vices as for the drab mediocrity which they foster. Rameau differs from the society that has spawned him in that he is frank and honest in his opinions, but he shows himself to be its true son in his inability to raise himself to greatness. He and all the rest who accept the values of that society are condemned to dance the vile pantomime of beggary, subservience and parasitism which reduces its participants to an endless anguish of sterility and unfulfilment. As an artist no less than as a moralist he is a failure; however remarkable his talents as a mime, they place him at two removes from the truly creative musician. The possible genius has been destroyed by the ne'er-do-well. At the end of the dialogue the ambiguity that has surrounded Lui falls away; he in turn has been finally demasked by Moi.

The paths traced by the two protagonists of *Le Neveu de Rameau* are in precisely inverse relation to one another. Lui starts out lamenting his own mediocrity and indecisiveness. Moi, on the other hand, enters the conversation the very model of confident single-mindedness, unassailed by doubt or confusion. As the discussion proceeds the two characters change places; Lui comes to look upon himself as a happy rogue with claims to greatness, whereas it is now Moi's turn to show all the signs of mental turmoil and lack of self-confidence. In the last stage of the dialogue the situation is reversed once again, but it is not a simple return to the status quo. Rameau, finally convinced by Moi, resigns himself to his role as a mediocrity, consoling himself with the thought that it has not cost him much. Moi reaches a new serenity having reconciled himself to the fact that the neat moral and philosophical formulae which so easily sprang to his lips cannot encapsulate the inconsistency and unpredictability of human nature. Instead of keeping the world at bay behind a solidly constructed wall of doctrinaire beliefs, a moral vision which purports to lead men to happiness and fulfilment must enter the world and meet men as individuals at the point of their need. Diderot-Moi is only at the beginning of a process which will revamp his whole approach to morality. The way ahead is unclear, his encounter with Rameau has given him 'furiously to think'; but its successful conclusion shows him to be on the right lines.

In the last resort the outcome of the debate in *Le Neveu de Rameau* as I have interpreted it over the preceding pages hinges on the drawing of a character so powerfully conceived in his individuality as to be totally impregnable to reductionist formulae of any sort. Socially, morally and psychologically it must be rendered impossible to label him as a type. In the creation of Rameau as both an eccentric and a rogue Diderot succeeded masterfully in meeting all these conditions, and in so doing created one of the most remarkable characters in French fiction. Not until Balzac was French fiction again to have an author with an imagination capable of giving birth to characters of such overwhelming energy and convincing singularity.

Socially Rameau is an outsider, a wandering Jew of Parisian society who trades his talents where he may but never gains acceptance in any group. The very range of his social acquaintances, from coachman to government minister, is a sure sign in a highly stratified society of a failure to find a niche. He does not even fit into the category of social parasite completely since there are limits beyond which he will not go in the pursuit of a comfortable bed, warm clothes and good food. Rameau's social ostracism is the consequence of his moral heterodoxy; he refuses to adhere to the code of any group. For him the practice of virtue is a worthless folly dreamed up by woolly-minded idealists, but he is incapable of the kind of hypocrisy and self-abasement which would ensure him a sinecure in the cynical world of the men with position and power. In a conflict-oriented society such a show of independence from the two opposing ideological groupings is intolerable to either. He is despised by the man of virtue for throwing in his lot with the moral nihilism that rules the established order, and he is spurned by the villain for failing to be complete in his depravity. Reviled as a moral delinquent in the eyes of those who inhabit separate ends of the ethical scale his roguery is absolute, and since there appears to be no one like him, complete. Rameau is the quintessential rogue in whom one might almost say roguery is raised to the level of a metaphysics. His delinquency is his refusal to recognize any order, meaning or final redemption outside himself. Not that he conceives of himself in these terms, at least not at first. He desperately wants to belong, to fit in. His express purpose in life is to practise his vice within the framework of recognized conventions, raising it to such a level of refinement that its transcendent artistry will provoke the respect and admiration of others. Through his very roguery he seeks the approbation and acceptance of others which will draw him into the fabric of the community. His failure to achieve his aim has the effect of heightening the individuality of a character which foils all attempts, even those of its owner, to establish it within a moral and social category.

The ultimate demonstration of Rameau's irreducibility as a unique human being vis-à-vis any philosophy or doctrine is his own failure to explain away his personality in terms of a dogmatic biological materialism. He asserts that the causes of his moral insensitivity can be traced to a hereditary deficiency within his physiological constitution: 'Some things need a sense I don't possess, a fibre that hasn't been vouchsafed me, or a slack one that you can tweak as much as you like but it won't vibrate. . . . The paternal molecule must be hard and obtuse, and this wretched first molecule has affected everything else' (pp. 107–8). This deficiency, he believes, has been passed on to his son, and it would be pointless his trying to counteract the genetically determined bent towards vice in his offspring. Rameau's materialism is of the most resolutely determinist kind. Modification of the personality through self-discipline, education or social pressure is doomed to fail in the face of sheer biological necessity. The only effect of such factors is to divide a man against himself and deprive him of the happiness which is the certain fruit of his compliance with the requirements of his inner nature.

If Rameau's explanation of his own motives for action were true he would be no more than a complex machine programmed to react to any given situation in a predictable way. The understanding of human personality is in his philosophy reduced to the laws of mechanics; its ineffability is a myth. Yet doubts arise when the definition is compared with the object defined. Rameau is not the 'thief happy to be among wealthy thieves' that he claims he is. He has been forced to execute a swift exit from the Bertin-Hus household because for once he has dared to show 'a bit of taste, intelligence and reason'. He knows that this brief rejection of his abject condition goes against what he holds to be his inner nature, but something within him prevents him from going back and going through with the debasing humiliation which would be demanded of him in return for the restoration of his creature comforts: 'It can't be done. (Placing his right hand on his heart): I can feel something there rising in revolt and saying: "Rameau, you will do nothing of the kind". There must be a certain dignity connected with man's nature and which nothing can stifle' (p. 48). Stronger than his physical needs and the inclinations of his temperament there exists within Rameau an ineradicable need to maintain his personal integrity. A man who prostitutes his dignity will lose his self-respect, his humanity and his sense of individual existence.

In his heart of hearts Rameau knows that if he constricts his personality by forcing it into rigid conformity with the dictates of his deterministic philosophy he will destroy himself. By trying to impose a perfect consistency on the existing order of things he is implicitly denying his own existence as an imperfect being incapable of maintaining that consistency in his own life. Rameau the dogmatist must give way to Rameau the man. 'The main thing,' he remarks to Moi, 'is that you and I should exist, and that we should be you and I. Apart from that let everything go as it likes. The best order of things, to my way of thinking, is the one I was meant to be part of, and to hell with the most perfect of worlds if I am not of it. I would rather exist, even as an impudent argufier, than not exist at all.' (pp. 42–3.) Heredity has contributed to the fashioning of the 'impudent argufier', but so has environment; his insensitivity to virtue and his artistic sterility are due at least in part to the company he keeps. Yet the man is more than the sum of his parts. He stands there irrational, inconsistent and unpredictable, defying all attempts, his own included, to circumscribe his personality with the inhuman logic of quasi-mathematical explanations.

At the end of the discussion Rameau leaves the stage of the Régence a chastened man. He has learnt that he has not and never will achieve greatness; but in his final exchange with Moi his defeat is outweighed by a higher consolation:

Lui: Good-bye, Mr. Philosopher. Isn't it true that I am always the same?
Moi: Alas, yes, unfortunately.
Lui: So long as I have that misfortune for another forty years! He laughs best who laughs last. (p. 125)

This is no face-saving bravado. He knows that he is a fool, but there is no other fool like him. It is his very folly which makes him irreplaceable. In the character of Rameau Diderot has demonstrated conclusively that sublimity in human affairs derives not from the cultivation of perfection but from the successful maintenance of the individual's uniqueness against the conforming pressures from within and without. An apt epitaph for Rameau would be the words written at the beginning of his *Confessions* by that other sublime fool, Jean-Jacques Rousseau: 'I am made unlike anyone I have ever met; I will even venture to say that I am like no one in the whole world. I may be no better but at least I am different'.[1] Like Jean-Jacques, Rameau never experiences the happiness of true fulfilment. Divided against himself he knows the anguish of self-contempt born of failure to achieve the ideal of perfection as he sees it. He does not enjoy the final fulfilment of the other delinquent figures of eighteenth-century fiction whose basic humanitarianism ensures their eventual repentance and the concomitant reward of material prosperity. Such a naïve optimism is absent from the pages of Diderot's work. Yet neither can it be said that tragedy lies at the heart of this study in delinquency. Rameau's suffering is real, but it is the sign and guarantee of his dignity and autonomy as a human being.

[1] *The Confessions*, trans. J. M. Cohen (Harmondsworth 1953), p. 17.

BIBLIOGRAPHY

Texts

DIDEROT, DENIS: *Le Neveu de Rameau*, édition critique avec notes et lexique par Jean Fabre (Geneva 1963).
— *Rameau's Nephew and D'Alembert's Dream*, trans. L. W. Tancock (Harmondsworth 1966).
— *Rameau's Nephew and Other Works*, trans. Jacques Barzun and Ralph H. Bowen (New York 1956).

Critical Works

DIDEROT, Denis:
Baricelli, Jean-Pierre: 'Music and the Structure of Diderot's *Le Neveu de Rameau*', *Criticism* V (1963) 95–111.
Crocker, Lester G.: '*Le Neveu de Rameau*, une expérience morale', *Cahiers de l'Association Internationale des Etudes Françaises* XIII (1961) 133–55.
Doolittle, James: *Rameau's Nephew, a Study of Diderot's 'Second Satire'*, (Paris-Geneva 1960).

Duchet, Michèle and Launay, Michel: *Entretiens sur 'Le Neveu de Rameau'* (Paris 1967).

Fellows, Otis E.: 'The Theme of Genius in Diderot's *Neveu de Rameau*', *Diderot Studies* II (1952) 168–99.

Grimsley, Ronald: 'Psychological Aspects of *Le Neveu de Rameau*', *MLQ* VI (1955) 195–209.

Josephs, Herbert: *Diderot's Dialogue of Gesture and Mime; 'Le Neveu de Rameau'* (Ohio 1969).

Kabelac, Sharon L.: 'Irony as a Metaphysics in *Le Neveu de Rameau*', *Diderot Studies* XIV (1970) 95–112.

Laufer, Roger: '*Le Neveu de Rameau*' in *Style Rococo, style des lumières* (Paris 1963).

Launay, Michel: 'Sur les intentions de Diderot dans *Le Neveu de Rameau*', *Diderot Studies* VIII (1966) 105–18.

Marsland, Amy S.: 'Identity and Theme in *Le Neveu de Rameau*', *RR* LX (1969) 34–46.

Plotkin, F.: 'Mime as pander: Diderot's *Neveu de Rameau*', *Studies on Voltaire and the Eighteenth Century* LXX (1970) 27–41.

Sandomirsky, Natalie L.: 'The Ethical Standard of the Genius in Diderot's *Neveu de Rameau*', *Symposium* XVIII (1964) 46–55.

T. E. LITTLE

Dead Souls

EXAMINING THE PLACE OF 'DEAD SOULS' AMONG EURO-
pean picaresque novels, one might arrive at the conclusion
that Gogol's novel cannot be called picaresque in the strict sense
of the word. F. D. Reeve expresses this opinion on the grounds that
the hero does not 'climb the social ladder'[1] and the Soviet critic
D. E. Tamarchenko puts the same argument into Marxist terms,
arguing that there is not sufficient contrast between the hero and
his environment, and that *Dead Souls* is in fact a denial and an
exposé of the picaresque tradition.[2] Janko Lavrin, however, describes it as following the pattern of the old picaresque novel[3] and
Marc Slonim considers it Gogol's intention to write a humorous
novel of this genre.[4]

Nevertheless, *Dead Souls* has not been included here under false
pretences because, although not one of the intimate family, it does
have the picaresque novel as an ancestor, together with other
genres. Professor E. M. Wilson has maintained that the English
novels of the eighteenth century cannot be reckoned picaresque in
the strict Spanish sense[5] and might be disposed to take a similar
view of this Russian novel, but all have strong affinities with the
tradition, and there are sufficient picaresque elements in *Dead Souls*
to justify its inclusion here.

Nikolai Gogol was born in 1809 and died in 1852. He was a

[1] F. D. Reeve: *The Russian Novel* (London 1967), p. 78.
[2] D. E. Tamarchenko: 'Myortvyye Dushi', *Istoriya Russkogo Romana* (Moscow-
Leningrad 1962, 2 vols.), Vol. I, p. 332.
[3] J. Lavrin: *An Introduction to the Russian Novel* (London 1947), p. 32.
[4] M. Slonim: *An Outline of Russian Literature* (London 1958), p. 68.
[5] *Cassell's Encyclopaedia of Literature*, ed. S. H. Steinberg (London 1953, 2 vols.),
Vol. I, p. 420.

strange creature, a man of bizarre habits and morbid temperament, the eccentricities of whose life have been described with appropriate humour by Vladimir Nabokov.[1] He had the strange childhood habit of piling furniture into the centre of the room and crowing like a cock on top of it, and even in adult life would write strange letters to his mother and friends in a style of remote fantasy, showing that for him the boundaries between dream and reality, fact and imagination, were decidedly blurred. This ran in the family, for his mother was also prone to some exotic fancies and at various times attributed to her son the invention of steamships and railroads. Gogol's death was as strange as his life. He expired from causes compounded of religious mania and medical treatment, having burnt most of what was to be part two of *Dead Souls,* some of which still survives in fragmentary form and which, apart from some vivid characterization, is marked inferior to part one.

Although a fairly prolific writer, this novel, which Gogol called a *poema* or epic poem, is his longest work, and immediately the title page raises questions not only about the classification of the book within the genre of the novel, but also about its very right to be considered as a novel at all.

Discussions on genre classification are tedious and frequently futile, for literature, as the living product of inventive human minds, does not submit easily to categories and the very existence of the novel is a testimony to nature's ability to produce hybrids from hitherto pure forms. Robert Liddell quotes Saintsbury to the effect that the history of the novel is identical with the history of the romance, whether in prose or verse. Fielding, in writing *Joseph Andrews,* was attempting a new art form called *comic-epic* and, until George Eliot restored unity of action as a principle, it was the exception in the English novel, apart from such authors as Jane Austen.[2] Gogol himself had a fairly fluid concept of genres. He considered that literature could be divided into two basic genres: the lyrical and the dramatic-narrative. In the first, the author conveys his own feelings and emotions as coming from himself, in the second he portrays other people and makes them perform and express emotions of their own.

This second genre, Gogol divides into three separate aspects:

[1] V. Nabokov: *Nikolai Gogol* (New York 1944).
[2] Robert Liddell: *A Treatise on the Novel* (London 1960), p. 14.

the novel, the epic and the minor epic. The subject of an epic would be the life of an entire nation or an epoch in the history of humanity. A novel would be concerned with one particular incident in life and a minor epic would depict everything of note in the features and customs of the particular time chosen by the author for consideration. The three sub-genres are distinguished too by the nature of their heroes. The hero of an epic would be a remarkable and distinctive personage and the hero of a novel could be of little importance, while in a minor epic the hero would be a person of no particular eminence, but distinctive in many respects.[1]

Tamarchenko points out the artificiality of Gogol's divisions and shows that the features Gogol ascribes to the minor epic can be applied to the eighteenth-century English novel.[2] It is not our purpose here to seek a final definition of the novel, but it is sufficient for present purposes to stress that in Gogol's thought, and in general literary criticism, the novel is closely linked to the drama and to the epic, the divisions being indistinct enough at the time for us to consider Gogol's poem as a novel. Pushkin in *Yevgeny Onegin* had written a novel in verse and it was a pleasing gesture on Gogol's part to reverse the procedure and write a poem in prose. As the author of an epic poem, albeit a very bad one, *Gants Kyukhel'garten*, and of a brilliant play, *The Inspector General*, Gogol's own literary activity reflects the mixed history of the novel.

If the problem of definition is still found troublesome, one can follow the example of E. M. Forster and take refuge in Abel Chevalley's definition of the novel as 'une fiction en prose d'une certaine étendue',[3] which will grant *Dead Souls* entry into the company of novels, if one forgets that Gogol's prose with its colour, rhythm and melody hovers on the verge of poetry![4]

Dead Souls was written between 1836 and 1841 while Gogol was resident in Western Europe, chiefly Italy and France, and was published in 1842. The title requires perhaps some explanation for those unfamiliar with conditions in nineteenth-century Russia. At

---

[1] N. V. Gogol: *Polnoye Sobraniye Sochineniy* (AN SSSR, Leningrad 1952, 14 vols.), Vol. VIII, pp. 477–9.
[2] D. E. Tamarchenko: op. cit., p. 330.
[3] E. M. Forster: *Aspects of the Novel* (Penguin Books, Harmondsworth 1968), p. 13.
[4] Professor Gifford's comment that *Dead Souls* was rightly called a poem because 'it cannot be translated without losing much' is a little superficial (H. Gifford: *The Novel in Russia* (London 1964), p. 43).

that time peasants were bought and sold by the landowners much as we sell cars and furniture today, and like houses and estates, they could also be mortgaged. It was one of the quaintnesses of the system that these negotiable people were referred to as *souls*, so if a landowner said he owned five hundred souls, this meant he was overlord of five hundred peasant slaves. Every landowner had to pay tax on his peasants and a census was taken every five years to determine how many serfs a man possessed. If a peasant died during this five-year period, the owner had to continue paying tax on him until the next census, and thus the dead lived on as phantoms among the bureaucrats.

The hero of the novel, Pavel Ivanovich Chichikov, has found a splendid scheme for extorting money from the government. He visits various landowners and offers to buy their dead souls, i.e., to effect a sale on paper. The landowner would, in theory, be pleased that somebody should relieve him of the burden of paying tax on his dead, non-productive peasants and Chichikov benefits from the deal by using these serfs he has purchased on paper to raise a mortgage from the government. In fact this was an implausible scheme because legally serfs could only be sold with their families and so the plot of the novel is also implausible. This is a grave shortcoming in the novel overlooked by those who consider it a political satire, but from the literary point of view, the implausibility is of little significance. The important thing is to get Mr. Chichikov around and about in search of gullible landowners.

The novel opens with Chichikov's arrival at the town in his coach and ends with his riding out propelled by a gust of lyrical hot air from the narrator. Between these events he visits a veritable zoo of landowners and we observe the way in which he broaches his macabre request to each one. Having completed negotiations for the transfer of the serfs, Chichikov returns to the town to register his purchases officially. In the eyes of the townsfolk he has now become a person of enormous consequence and they invite him to the town ball, but there he meets his downfall, for one of the landowners, a garrulous drunkard called Nozdryov, reveals to the unsuspecting assembly that all Chichikov's serfs, on which they had based their ideas of his enormous wealth, are in fact dead men.

Rumour and speculation fill the town and the ludicrous idea grows up that Chichikov is scheming to elope with the daughter of the provincial governor and the purchase of the peasants is a mere cover. Feeling that things are getting too warm for him, Chichikov flees.

There are many points here in common with the picaresque tradition. Chichikov is a rogue and a swindler, bent on improving his status by crooked means and, in achieving his end, he does the rounds of what, at first glance, appears to be a cross-section of Russian provincial society: landowners, peasants, bureaucrats and townsmen. The novel is episodic in construction. The chapters dealing with Chichikov's visits to the landowners are tableaux linked loosely together by the presence and the interpolations of the author, in his capacity as narrator. Suspense and tension give the novel a technical unity as the reader is not told until the end precisely why Chichikov wants dead serfs. This is not to imply, as Lavrin unintentionally seems to do, that the plot's structure is artistically weak.[1] It is, on the contrary, well-planned with a grand climax at the end to provide fitting proof of Gogol's dramatic abilities.

Like many picaresque novels the book is humorous, although this might not come over so well in translation, depending as it does on tricks of vocabulary and syntax which are very difficult to render into English. Apart from this, the humour requires for its appreciation an inbuilt relish for the absurd and the sick which many readers will find distasteful.

There is considerable emphasis on the squalid and sordid in *Dead Souls*, but it is not the sexual or excremental humour that one finds in Grimmelshausen's *Simplicius Simplicissimus*. Nevertheless, there is something faintly disgusting about the novel which one senses but cannot pinpoint. Most of the nastiness centres around Chichikov, about whom Gogol gives information of a peculiarly unclean kind. He changes his underwear once every other day in the winter and once a day in summer. When washing he scrubs his cheeks until they are satin smooth and tweeks little hairs from his nose. There are frequent references to insects. Cockroaches peer out like prunes from the walls of the inn and flies buzz merrily around. Smells of both objects and people are lovingly described and this leads to an excessive interest in noses, upon which Gogol

[1] J. Lavrin: op. cit., p. 32: 'The novel is built up on so slender a plot that it is devoid even of love intrigue'.

also lavishes careful attention. Chichikov blows his with a pleasing trumpeting sound and thus excites the admiration and respect of dining room waiters, and on one occasion his snores mingle with those of his two servants to form a musical trio.

Part of Gogol's corporological obsession centres around haemorrhoids and we are told once that Chichikov fell into a sound sleep which only happy mortals enjoy who know nothing of haemorrhoids, or fleas, or strongly developed intellectual faculties.

There are links here with the broad picaresque tradition, but there are also divergencies from it of greater or lesser significance. Although a swindler, Chichikov is not a servant or underdog and is not, at first sight, a social drop-out. Far from being at odds with his environment, fighting furiously for a living, Chichikov lives in accord with provincial society and is received by its members with rapture because he is so charming. He is not a reject, but an ultra-respectable man and his aim in buying the dead serfs is as much personal gain as social advancement.

These are weighty arguments and are given partial support by Tamarchenko to support his contention that *Dead Souls* does not stand in the picaresque tradition, but much depends on one's interpretation of a social drop-out. It is true that most of the other characters in *Dead Souls* are rogues, but characters in the more orthodox picaresque novels are scarcely remarkable for their shining honesty. Chichikov *is* at war with his environment in that he is deliberately exploiting its values for the purpose of deception. His activities are illegal and therefore at odds with established order, an argument that should have some attraction for Soviet critics. It is no argument to assert that as serf-owning is now recognized to be immoral Chichikov's misdeeds can now be reckoned as a cavalier's strategy in battle with a criminal state, for Chichikov does not see himself in such a light. Reeve's contention that *Dead Souls* is not picaresque because Chichikov 'does not climb the social ladder' is unconvincing.[1] The potted biography of Chichikov at the end of the novel makes it quite clear that he has sought comfort and status all his life and his encounters with other people in the book are marked by a chameleon-like ability to ingratiate himself into anybody's favour. Not only is he physically travelling around the country but climbing up carefully into universal esteem.

[1] F. D. Reeve: op. cit., p. 78.

Another objection which could be made to the classification of the novel as picaresque is the relatively little amount of action. The subtitle of the book, *The Adventures of Chichikov*, is misleading and was imposed on Gogol by the censor on the grounds that as souls were immortal they could not correctly be described as dead.

Compared to the Spanish picaresque heroes and to Moll Flanders or Roderick Random, Chichikov has relatively few adventures, although in the second part of the book there are more events. In the first part of the novel, however, the encounters are of Chichikov's own choosing and as he trundles around the country in search of dead souls, the reader's curiosity is stirred not so much by the question of what will befall him next as by what will he *do* next and why does he want dead serfs anyway? It is difficult to find a yardstick with which to measure action in a novel but here, although incidents do not follow one another apace, the book does not lack activity, since all Chichikov's interviews with the landowners are carefully conducted and skilful man-oeuvres, the march and countermarch of Chichikov's tactics being as exciting as physical action. A quarrel with the loud and aggres-sive Nozdryov and the latter's inopportune appearance at the ball supply some of the few incidents which come as unexpected and catastrophic shocks to the hero.

It is true that Chichikov is not a servant in bondage to a series of masters like the Spanish picaresque heroes, but morally he is perhaps little better than they, since he is a fawning and cringing creature who bows and scrapes with sweet politeness to anybody who can help him on his way to self-advancement.

Unlike other picaresque novels *Dead Souls* is not an autobiog-raphy, but nevertheless it is a first-person narrative, for Gogol, in probable imitation of Sterne, Cervantes, Fielding and others, has complete control of the narration and often digresses from it to discourse on matters which are, strictly speaking, irrelevant to the plot. It is Gogol who supplies Chichikov's biography from early childhood up to the present day. This account is one of only two such biographies given by Gogol about the characters appearing in the novel. In a more orthodox picaresque production, Chichikov's life would have constituted the actual book, whereas *Dead Souls* is an episode in Chichikov's career. It might be argued that the book is only the first part of an intended trilogy, but in view of the

the fact that only the first part has come down to us whole and the unlikelihood of Gogol's being capable of finishing the rest anyway, the first part of *Dead Souls* must be judged as it stands.

A serious break with the picaresque tradition and indeed with most traditional literature, is the complete absence of love interest or of any sexual encounters. Chichikov himself is sexless and the female characters are mere parodies of femininity, and when obliged to depict them, Gogol avoids even superficial characterization but takes refuge in grotesque simile or cliché. Most of his young women are as white-skinned and as fresh as fresh can be, beautiful as the day is long. One glides into the narrative like a swan, another is compared to a rich juicy turnip, another stands upright like a palm tree and yet another, for whom Gogol feels the travesty of affection, has a face like a freshly boiled egg. Young women did not interest Gogol much in life and they receive perfunctory treatment in his works. The female landowner, Korobochka, is the only feminine character in *Dead Souls* whose characterization stands out with any sharpness.

These are comparatively minor points, but as a picaresque novel *Dead Souls* has one significant shortcoming. Despite the wide variety of picaresque offspring in European literature, all the novels in this series have one thing in common. In describing the adventures of the hero or heroine the author has given us a picture of contemporary society, usually in its more squalid form, frequently making the novel a study in low life. Individual authors depict society for a number of reasons, tendentiously with a view to encouraging reform or merely accurately, with no political or social axe-grinding. A description of society is often subsidiary to the development of a human situation or to the demands of an entertaining plot. Whatever the reason, nobody has doubted that contemporary society is being portrayed, although the emphasis of the author and subsequent critics may vary. But whatever the emphasis of author or critic, the accurate, if comic or grotesque, depiction of society is an important feature of the picaresque novel.

What about *Dead Souls*? There has been no shortage of critics who proclaim it a work of social and political satire. It was hailed as such by contemporary critics who saw in it a merciless attack on Tsarist Russia and serfdom. Belinsky, the supreme pontiff of Russian criticism whose encyclicals are read with more reverence than anything which ever came from the Vatican, informed his readers that Gogol was the first Russian writer to look boldly and directly into Russian reality. This attitude was adopted by most critics until the beginning of the century and it is still a widely held view in Soviet criticism. Mashinsky has written of Gogol's sympathy for the enslaved people[1] and Tamarchenko even denies *Dead Souls* the classification of picaresque on the grounds that it was socially critical whereas the eighteenth-century English novels were merely socially descriptive.[2] The symbolists and formulists in Russia at the beginning of the century attempted to correct this view. Eykhenbaum writes in 1924 that critics have been too long hypnotized by Belinsky.[3] Trubitsin's statement that critics must stop looking at Gogol through the eyes of Belinsky[4] is severely denied by Gukovsky.[5] British and American critics have also been divided on the subject. W. Phelps in 1911 describes *Dead Souls* as the first of the great realistic novels of Russia and applauds Gogol's photographic reality.[6] Professor Seeley in 1968 has identified Chichikov's frauds with the acquisitive spirit of capitalism, as though greed did not exist under other economic systems.[7] Vladimir Nabokov, on the other hand, devotes his entire book to the mockery of any realistic or political interpretation of Gogol and impresses upon his readers the significant fact that Gogol was born on April 1st. Dmitri Chizhevsky has also spoken against the idea of Gogol as a realist, on the grounds that *reality* is a relative term which is understood differently by different people at different times and can have no absolute validity.[8]

Two questions are to be resolved here. Did Gogol have any explicit social and political convictions which he sought to embody in his writings and, if he did, are his works a successful expression of them?

About Gogol's 'revolutionary' opinions there is little to be said.

[1] S. Mashinsky: *Gogol' i revolyutsionnyye demokraty* (Moscow 1953), p. 7.
[2] D. E. Tamarchenko: op. cit., p. 33.
[3] B. M. Eykhenbaum: 'Kak sdelana Shinel' Gogolya', *Skvoz' Literaturu* (Leningrad 1924), pp. 191–2.
[4] N. Trubitsin: 'Idealizm Gogolya', *Russkiy Filologicheskiy Vestnik* No. 1 (April 1909), p. 299.
[5] G. Gukovsky: *Realizm Gogolya* (Moscow-Leningrad 1959), p. 392.
[6] W. Phelps: *Essays on Russian Novelists* (New York 1911), pp. 51–56.
[7] F. F. Seeley: 'Gogol's *Dead Souls*', *FMLS* IV (1968) 33–44.
[8] D. Chizhevsky: 'The Unknown Gogol', *Sl Rev* XXX (1951/2), 476–93.

Neither his letters nor his life reveal anything remotely resembling political or social preoccupations while engaged on his major works. Apart from his correspondence, there is the testimony of at least one friend that Gogol was apolitical,[1] and there is not a shred of evidence to prove that he was at any time opposed to the political and social evils, such as serfdom, which *Dead Souls* was reckoned to condemn. In 1847, Gogol published his last and weirdest work, *Selected Passages from a Correspondence with Friends*, in which he offered spiritual guidance to his friends including sage advice on the management of serfs. Among other things, the correct way of addressing a peasant is reckoned to be 'Hey you, with the dirty snout!'

The work provoked the fury of Gogol's former admirers who were annoyed that Gogol was not the progressive man they thought him to be. Some critics have tried to represent the book as a dramatic *volte-face* from the liberal views of *Dead Souls*, but this verges on academic dishonesty because Gogol's reactionary political views, which he combined with religious mysticism, were formed before he wrote the novel and his dramatic *volte-face* concerned more his attitude to the rôle and function of art than his attitude to political questions. The few 'social' theories he developed concerning literature were not exactly progressive, and in any case, as Paul Debreczeny proves, Gogol's theorising began *after* he wrote his works, a process which Nabokov calls 'planning in retrospect'.[2]

It is, therefore, difficult to regard *Dead Souls* as a political indictment of Tsarist society. This erroneous interpretation springs from naïve sociological considerations which have disastrous consequences when applied to literature. Serfdom, critics rightly considered, was an appalling evil, and therefore an author who portrays landowners and serfs in grotesque fashion must be protesting against the system. Such critics are too solemn to appreciate that external phenomena are merely raw material for a writer's creative processes and there are uses to which one can put this material other than the demand for social reform. For Gogol, all external phenomena were metamorphosed to satisfy his strongly

---

[1] P. A. Vyazemsky: *Polnoye Sobraniye Sochineniy* (St. Petersburg 1878, 12 vols.), Vol. I, pp. 273–5.
[2] Paul Debreczeny: 'Nikolai Gogol and his Contemporary Critics', *Transactions of the American Philosophical Society* (Philadelphia, April 1966), p. 23.

developed sense of the absurd, the incongruous or the grotesque. He used the external trappings of nineteenth-century Russia because he happened to live in that country at that time and it is ridiculous to transpose our views of social justice into the mind of a man who had different views and a different purpose. If, in a future age, the killing of animals for meat is considered barbarous, will Beatrix Potter's books be regarded as tendentious works in the struggle for vegetarianism, thus giving Flopsy Bunny the splendour of a social pioneer? Is the imperious conduct of the Red Queen in *Alice Through the Looking Glass* a protest against Autocracy? Carroll had, significantly enough, spent several weeks in Russia before he wrote the work, and such an interpretation of his book would be no less ludicrous than the accepted social and political interpretations of Gogol.

If we cannot accept Gogol as an enemy of political wrongs, let us consider his abilities as a faithful recorder of his *milieu*. Soviet critics have now largely discarded the view of Gogol as a committed political thinker but nevertheless cling to the assertion that he portrayed society accurately if grotesquely. Gukovsky declares that Gogol was an expression of the wrath of the peasant class, 'whether he liked it or not',[1] which is for us a splendid example of a critic making his author toe the line marked out for him.

Disagreement with the view that Gogol was an accurate depicter of his day and age was expressed very early in his career when a reviewer of his *Evenings on a Farm near Dikanka* complained of the 'facelessness' of his characters.[2] Another reader from the Ukraine complained that these same stories were full of errors regarding the customs of Ukrainian peasants they purported to be describing.[3] Of course, from the point of view of literature, ethnographical description is not really important, but such criticism is significant when an author is reckoned to be a faithful portrayer of national life. *Sorochinskiy Fair* contains linguistic and factual errors.

---

[1] G. Gukovsky: op. cit., pp. 473–4.
[2] *Severnaya Pchela*, No. 73 (1835), quoted by Paul Debreczeny, op. cit., p. 9.
[3] *Syn Otechestva* Vol. XXV (1832), quoted by Debreczeny, op. cit., p. 6. The strangeness of Gogol's characterizations is evident in his play *The Inspector General* and attracted the attention of V. Androssov, who was the only critic at the time to draw attention to the fantastic nature of Gogol's art without at the same time accusing him of caricature and exaggeration—the line of attack adopted by Gogol's enemies (*Moskovskiy Nablyudatel*, No. 1 (Moscow 1836), p. 125).

The fair itself was being held at a season when no peasant would have been able to attend it and many of the Ukrainian terms used by Gogol to describe food and clothes, making the tale so rich in *local colour*, Gogol had, in a fit of absent-mindedness, invented. This does not inspire confidence in Gogol as a portrayer of Russian actuality, especially when one considers that *Dead Souls* was written during the twelve years that Gogol spent abroad, and his knowledge of provincial Russia was anyway scanty. He had grown up on a small estate in the Ukraine, and most of his time in Russia was spent in and around the capital. Moreover, much of this period abroad was spent in Rome, where Gogol frequented the company of pious friends and underwent a deepening of his own religious convictions. No supporter of Gogol as a radical Russian realist has yet given a convincing explanation of how this progressive social and political satire was written while its author was developing religious notions in the notably unprogressive states of Pope Gregory XVI.[1]

An examination of the text of *Dead Souls* reveals the unreality of his characterization. It is apparent that Gogol's humour and scintillating imagery conceal a total inability to create solid human beings. Instead Gogol fobs the reader off with picturesque monsters born of imagination rather than observation. An example of this is the young lady with the face like a boiled egg whom we meet again in Chapter 8 at the ball:

The governor's wife who stood before him was not alone; on her arm was a fresh-looking fairhaired sixteen-year-old girl with delicate and graceful features, a pointed chin, an enchantingly rounded oval face, such that an artist might have taken as a model for a madonna and which is found only rarely in Russia, where everything, whatever it may be, likes to assume large proportions; mountains, woods, steppes, faces, lips and feet.

Here Gogol's *description* consists of hackneyed similes and a minor digression on Russian scenery grotesquely juxtaposed with physical anatomy. About the girl as a human being with a living psychology we know nothing, but the use of bathos as a humorous

[1] David Magarshak gives an interesting account of Gogol's sojourn in Rome (D. Magarshak: *Gogol, a life* (London 1957), pp. 158–62).

device and as a means of avoiding proper characterization is an astoundingly bold artistic technique.

Frequently in Gogol's characterizations, an inanimate object or an abstract quality will swallow up a character and then actually become the character. We are familiar with the technique of giving a character a single _leit-motif_ or single characteristic: Athene of the flashing eyes in Homer's _Odyssey_ or the little princess with down on her lip in Tolstoy's _War and Peace_. Gogol, in conscious or unconscious parody, awards most of his characters a physical or moral _leit-motif_ which subsequently dominates and swallows up the person. This may be called the technique of the mask and it was against such unreal distortions of mankind that Dostoyevsky protests in his story _Poor Folk_ in which Dostoyevsky's poor clerk, Devushkin, is outraged by the gross travesty of humanity represented by Gogol's poor clerk, Akaky Akakevich in _The Overcoat_.

Chichikov's _leit-motif_ is smoothness and, as Mirsky puts it, his geometrical expression is roundness.[1] Everything Gogol says about him is a variation on the theme of roundness and smoothness. He has chubby, satin-smooth cheeks and chubby little buttocks. He is compared to a little rubber ball and his gait is a bounce. Regularly he sponges his smooth little body with water and Eau de Cologne and his speech is as smooth as his appearance and manners.

Korobochka, the only female landowner, has boxness as her motif, with archaism as a subsidiary theme. Her name means 'little box' and everything about her is a lunatic continuation of the box theme, with things enclosed in other things. Her mirrors, Gogol carefully points out, are enclosed in heavy frames, and behind them are envelopes. She hoards away money in hundreds of little bags enclosed in lots of little drawers. Her food is a riot of stuffed dishes:

> Chichikov looked round and saw that the table was already spread with mushrooms, pies, fried eggs, curd tarts, potato cakes, stuffed pancakes and pasties with a variety of different fillings, some with onions, some with poppy seeds [themselves containers! TEL], some with curds and some with fish and God only knows with what else.

[1] D. Mirsky: _A History of Russian Literature_, ed. and abridged by Francis J. Whitfield (New York 1960), p. 153.

Sobakevich, whose name is derived from the word *sobaka*, meaning 'dog', is compared to a medium-sized bear. His *leit-motif* is animal largeness and coarseness. He is surrounded by pictures of large healthy men to match his large healthy character, and his furniture zealously takes after him. Each item is large and ungainly and every chair and table seems to say 'I too am Sobakevich' or 'I am very much like Sobakevich'. In the description of all these characters, speech, furniture, the outer appearance of their houses, children, servants and wives are all subservient to the one motif. This policy is carried through with a thoroughness that makes the reader suspect the author's intentions, and it seems clear that the aim is not the description of the world as it is, but the exploitation of a comic theme.

Speech is highly important in this respect and in each of the major characters it is idiomatic and distinctive. Manilov, the first landowner Chichikov meets, has cloying sweetness as his motif. His name is cleverly chosen for its association with the noun *malina* (raspberry) and the verb *manit'* (to lure, entice). Both he and his wife converse in diminutives and superlatives in order to express their exquisite joy and tenderness towards each other and Chichikov, the arch-chameleon, readily gets the hang of their idiom. His farewell to Mrs. Manilov is a brilliant imitation of his hosts' style:

'Madam, here,' he laid his hand on his heart, 'yes, it is here that the delightful time I have spent with you will be treasured for ever. And, believe me, there can be no greater bliss than to live with you, if not in the same house, then in the closest vicinity.' 'But you know, Pavel Ivanovich,' said Manilov, to whom this idea had the utmost appeal, 'it would indeed be a most excellent idea if we could live together under one roof, or in the shade of some elm tree where we could philosophize a while on anything under the sun and delve deep into the mysteries of life.' 'Ah, paradise itself,' said Chichikov with a sigh. 'Good-bye Madam,' he went on, going up to Mrs. Manilov and kissing her hand. 'Good-bye, my most estimable friend.'

English does not possess the prefixes and suffixes needed to convey the nauseating sentimentality of Manilov's speech. But although distinctive, this is not the speech of real people. It is very funny but highly stylised, and lacks the nuances of human conversation, for as with most things Gogolian, the important thing is the joke, not plot or genuine characterization.

Characterization is often achieved by a variety of linguistic jokes involving plays on symmetry or contrast. Our first introduction to Chichikov is conducted in a series of balanced negative contrasts which cancel each other out to make a genuine non-entity:

The gentleman in the carriage was not handsome, but neither was he particularly bad-looking; he was neither too fat nor too thin; he could not be said to be old, but he was not too young either.

An extension of this method involves two people when the author can use the mirror technique to make one the exact replica, or the exact contrast, of the other. Lewis Carroll uses it with Tweedledum and Tweedledee, but in one of Gogol's short stories, *The Story of How Ivan Ivanovich Quarrelled with Ivan Nikiforich,* the two heroes, unlike Carroll's, resemble a man and his image reflected in a *distorting* mirror. One man is very thin and has a face like a radish with the tail turned up, the other is very fat with a face like a radish with the tail turned down. Technically, Tweedledum and Tweedledee are enantiomorphs, related to one another as an object is to its image in a mirror.[1] So are Bobchinsky and Dobchinsky, two men with fat little tummies in Gogol's *The Inspector General.* There is doubtless a technical term to express the geometrical distortion of the two Ivans, but all these characters are the products of minds which delight in the rearrangement of objects and concepts to conform with a private relish for topsy turvydom. This is amusing if such humour is to one's taste, but a joke founded on gemoetrical devices and given a touch of the grotesque by unexpected vegetable imagery is in no way serious literary characterisation of human beings.

It is curious how certain critics are too dull to sense the pleasure which such intellectual and linguistic games can give an author and his readers simply for their own sake. Not content with the joke, such critics must seek out hidden meanings or some *significance* that will fit in with their own solemn fads. The quarrel of the two Ivans

[1] See M. Gardner: *The Annotated Alice* (Penguin Books, Harmondsworth 1970), p. 231.

is proclaimed a masterly study of decay and boredom in Tsarist Russia, an inevitable consequence of autocracy. When in *The London Mercury* of July 1933 we find Shane Leslie identifying *Alice in Wonderland* as a secret history of religious controversy in Victorian Oxford[1] (orange marmalade = William of Orange) we can hope that the critic is joking, but other critics advance ludicrous notions with appalling seriousness. If Soviet critics can be reproached for allowing political commitments to obscure their literary judgements, Western critics confuse literary issues with pseudo-psychology and sex. Natalia Kolb-Seletski in a recent article says comparatively little about Gogol's use of food as a device for humour and characterization, but makes much of her solemn theory, backed by psycho-analytical data, that food in Gogol's works is a substitute for sex.[2] Lewis Carroll has suffered from critics who think his affection for little girls somehow affects the literary merit of *Alice in Wonderland*.

Gogol's ability to construct non-entities is truly remarkable. Chichikov himself is a chameleon whose character is largely determined by his surroundings, but another brilliant form of non-characterization is seen at the description of Sobakevich's dinner table. Four people sit down to eat, but the fourth is described thus:

> In the fourth place there very soon appeared—it is hard to say definitely who—whether a married lady, or a girl, a relation, a housekeeper or simply someone living in the house—a thing without a cap, about thirty years old, in a bright-coloured handerchief. There are persons who exist in the world not as primary objects but as incidental spots or specks on objects.

Gogol's art is uncanny in this ability to produce negatives with all the force of positives. He thus refutes Belgion's assertion that a novelist is not a creative artist because, according to Belgion, to create means 'to bring into existence out of nothing'.[3] In this respect, Gogol was probably the greatest creative artist ever.

Frequently, Gogol does not even go through the motions of

---

[1] 'Lewis Carroll and the Oxford Movement', *The London Mercury* XXVIII (July 1933), 233–9.

[2] 'Gastronomy, Gogol and his Fiction', *SRev* XXIX, No. 1 (1970) 35–57.

[3] Quoted by Robert Liddell, op. cit., p. 14. In the present writer's experience even careful readers of *Dead Souls* will put the number of people at Sobakevich's table as three.

characterization but simply wanders away at a tangent from the character under discussion and by the time he has returned to the narrative, the reader has forgotten that Gogol was meant to be describing somebody. We have seen an illustration of this in the case of the girl with the egg face, but a more frequent method of avoiding the point is the vulgarization of the Homeric simile. One is familiar with the way in which Homer brings his similes to life until they become scenes in their own right. In the *Iliad* Agamemnon addresses an assembly of Greeks:

> Agamemnon's words went straight to the heart of every man in the crowd and the whole assembly was stirred like the waters on the Icarian sea when a southeaster falls on them from a lowering sky and sets the great waves on the move, or like deep corn in a tumbled field bowing its ears to the onslaught of the wild West Wind.[1]

With Homer these similes add beauty to his poetry, and in this case he implies that there is a connection between the grandeur of the wind and sea and the grandeur of Agamemnon's army.

Gogol's similes are less lofty in their function. As Chichikov approaches Sobakevich's house:

> He noticed two faces peering simultaneously out of the window ... a woman's face in a bonnet as long and narrow as a cucumber, and a man's as full and round as the Moldavian Pumpkins, the so-called 'flagons' out of which balalaikas are made in Russia, light two-stringed balalaikas, the pride and joy of the jaunty twenty-year-old peasant dandy, winking and whistling at the white-breasted and white-throated village maidens who gather round to listen to his soft strummings. No sooner had the two faces popped out than they vanished.

Here, two faces became pumpkins, vegetables for which Gogol seemed to harbour an unnatural affection, and then a balalaika, creating a bogus scene of village life, complete with supporting cast of village lads and lassies. All this in the time it takes two people to pop their heads out of the window and back again.

In Gogol's world, men can turn easily into vegetables or animals, or inanimate objects can become human. A man at the inn is indistinguishable from a samovar, Gogol says, except that he has

[1] Homer: *The Iliad*, trans. E. V. Rieu (Harmondsworth 1950), p. 43.

a large black beard. In Korobochka's house a turkey says 'bless you' to Chichikov, who tells it angrily not to be a damn fool.

There might be grounds for supposing Gogol to be a social observer if it could be shown that his own frequent interpolations into the narrative contained profound insights into the human situation. They do not. Most of his direct comments are in the vein of eloquent lunacy which duller lunatics have tried to take seriously. The description of the ball scene abounds in the sort of spurious description we have already discussed. An additional speciality is the delivery of outlandish generalizations in the tones of serious deliberation. Discussing the state of Chichikov's feelings towards the girl with the egg face, Gogol observes:

> One cannot say with any feeling of certainty whether the feeling of love had advanced in our hero's heart; it is indeed doubtful whether gentlemen of his kind, that is to say, not too fat, and yet not too thin, are capable of falling in love.

The illogic of this mockery disguises the fact that Gogol just could not depict human relationships in general. It is the most extraordinary feature of this unusual novel that, although made vivid and endowed with a monstrous life by the power of Gogol's language, the characters are all static. There are two attempts at filling in the past history of characters when Gogol relates the tale of Plyushkin's decline from a happy family man to a miser, and when he tells us of Chichikov's childhood. The first is unconvincing because the reader has the feeling that Gogol is out of his depth in trying to give an account of genuine psychological development, and it is one of the few occasions in the novel when the narrative flags and become boring.

The biography of Chichikov seems at first out of place because the long flashback to his past interrupts the flow of the novel. However, Gogol preserves his usual brilliant style in this account and it has a certain fascination because Gogol manages to explain Chichikov's character and at the same time preserve its static nature. Chichikov the child is as round and as smooth and as horrible as Chichikov the man. Like all Gogol's successful characterizations, he does not develop or change either in relation to the reader or in relation to the other characters in the novel. His creations stand in lurid grotesque splendour as though Bernini had tried his hand at modelling plastic gnomes. But it takes more than racy language and an eye for the sordid to make an author a realist, and to squeeze Gogol into this category by asserting that he is a realist, but in the grotesque manner, is avoiding the issue. An author who eschews human psychology, human conversation and the development of human relationships can only be called a *realist* by broadening the term to a point where it becomes meaningless. This is not to censure Gogol, for his genius lay in the realm of imagination, language and a sense of the ludicrous. Fortunately, we are not compelled to submit to the curious dogma that realism is the best or the ultimate form of literature.

It could be argued that Gogol's depiction of larger groups of society such as the bureaucracy and the scenes at the end involving the townsfolk are a realistic, if satirical, portrait of society. Here again such a view can only be based on the naïve assertion that a few so-called realistic details make an entire book or scene a realistic portrayal.

Gogol portrays his bureaucrats as inveterate bribe-takers, a fact that has been seized upon as an aspect of Gogol's slashing social satire, but even this we must see in proper perspective. Bribe-taking was such a common feature of Tsarist Russia that it was a thing on the same level as *tax fiddling* today, and in any case, it occupies a minor place in Gogol's picture. The dominant motif of the scene in the court president's office where Chichikov registers his purchase of the serfs is the elaborate comparison of the entire institution with the gods of Olympus. It seems that Gogol was reversing Homer's order of humour. The Greek poet had put his immortals into comically inappropriate situations. One remembers the troubles Aphrodite has during the siege of Troy when she imprudently abandons love-making to play at soldiers. Gogol, on the other hand, presents his horrible little mediocrities as gods, and the joke is sustained by the familiar Gogolian tricks of hyperbole and ludicrous illogic.

On his way to the court Chichikov meets Manilov and their delighted embrace and kiss last so long that both have toothache the rest of the day. Chichikov was not afraid of being late because the president of the court was a friend of his and could prolong or contract the business as Homer's Zeus could lengthen or shorten the days.

On entering the court, referred to elaborately as a temple of Themis (goddess of justice) a typical Gogolian spectacle awaits them:

Our heroes saw a prodigious number of papers, rough drafts and fair copies, bent heads, thick necks, dress coats, frock-coats of provincial cut, and even a light grey tunic which stood out conspicuously and which, turning its head on one side almost touching the paper, was copying out in a bold hand and with a flourish some official report of a successful lawsuit . . .

Note how the person has become a tunic. Some translators, not realizing the deliberate humour of this, have added a phrase such as 'the man who was wearing the tunic . . .'.[1] Reported conversation contains much deliberate bathos:

Brief sentences uttered by snatches and in a hoarse voice were audible from time to time, such as, 'Pray oblige me with Case No. 368, Feodosey Feodoseyvitch!' or, 'you are always mislaying the cork of the office ink-pot' . . . There was a great scratching of pens and the noise of it was like the passing of several carts loaded with brush-wood through a wood a quarter of a yard deep in dead leaves.

Leaving these phantom carts to plod through the narrative, this should be sufficient to show that the court office depicted by Gogol is the product of a vivid imagination taking as a starting point the commonly accepted, almost music-hall jokes of Russia that clerks took bribes and had scratchy pens. No acute observation is needed to state this, and Gogol's observation takes you no further. The rest of the so-called Portrait of Russian Life is built out of Gogol's sense of the absurd, which is here based chiefly on the incongruous association of literary ideas and the identification of these nonentities with classical heroes.

Chichikov and Manilov are conducted into the 'presence' by a temple votary

who had been offering sacrifices to Themis so diligently that both his sleeves had burst at the elbows and the lining was bulging out of the holes; for this he had been promoted to a higher rank. He rendered the same to our friends as Virgil had rendered to Dante. He took them into the president's office . . .

1 *Dead Souls*, trans. Constance Garnett (London 1922, 2 vols.), Vol. I, p. 216.

but in this place the new Virgil was so overwhelmed that he did not venture to set foot in it, but turned round, displaying his back worn as threadbare as a piece of matting and with a hen's feather clinging to it.

In Chapter 9, Gogol depicts a conversation between two women. It is important for the action of the book because it is during this conversation that the two ladies come, without any good reason, to the conclusion that Chichikov is planning to elope with the daughter of the provincial governor, and in coming to this crazy conclusion they set the whole town abuzz and create such a furore that Chichikov has to flee.

The ladies also are first-class examples of Gogol's ability to portray non-persons vividly. He refuses to give them names, only labels, and these labels cease to be labels and become by Gogolian alchemy the ladies themselves. Of the first lady, Gogol says:

Good taste marked every gesture; she was even fond of poetry and sometimes even knew how to hold her head dreamily, and everyone agreed that she was indeed a lady agreeable in all respects. The other lady, that is, the visitor, had not so versatile a character and we will call her, therefore, the merely agreeable lady! . . .

The conversation between agreeability in all respects and mere agreeability is an amusing and grotesque combination of sentimental frenchified speech and officialese. Apart from this, the only other attempts at characterization are not drawn from Gogol's observations of the feminine character, but from the general assumption that all women are natural gossips and all women are catty when talking about other women. This assumption might be true, but it requires more than humorous prejudice and clever parody to produce a study of women in society. If we accept this as such, we should have to accept Widow Twankey and Aladdin as a study in mother-son relationships in ancient China. The way in which Gogol depicts the town in uproar after the revelation of Chichikov's macabre purchases is a masterpiece of grand chaos. It is significant that Gogol does this by casting an almost supernatural aura of fantasy about the town, until it ceases to be a town as such, if it ever was one, but becomes a symbol of disruption and decay, primeval chaos and lurking evil. Gogol achieves this by having the town filled with mysterious characters with ludicrous names whom nobody knows and whom nobody has seen before. Highly unlikely, of course, but Gogol makes everything easier by quietly evacuating a position of omniscience and talking as though he is as perplexed as everybody else:

> Every inhabitant of the town stopped dead like a sheep with his eyes bulging out of his head. Dead Souls, the governor's daughter and Chichikov were all mixed and intermingled in their heads in a most extraordinary way . . . What was the point of these dead souls? There was no logic in dead souls. How do you buy dead souls? . . . The town that till then seemed to slumber peacefully suddenly was whipped as if by a whirlwind. All the sluggards and lie-abeds crawled out of their holes . . . it seemed that the town was both populous and large with its inhabitants. A Sysoy Parnutovich and a Macdonald Karlovich, who had never been heard of before suddenly made an appearance in public; a very long and lanky gentleman with an arm in a sling, taller than anybody who had ever been seen before, suddenly frequented the drawing rooms. All sorts of closed coaches, hitherto unknown traps, carriages that rattle and carriages with creaking wheels appeared in the streets and things began to get hot . . .

Gogol's ability to create a phantasmagorical city full of spook inhabitants galvanized into frantic activity by strange tales of dead souls, aroused much interest in later critics. The symbolists saw it as a representation of hell where the little demons (*melkiye besy*) are attracted by the activities of the Great Devil (*Glavnyy Chort*). Dostoyevsky seems to have imitated Gogol's technique of depicting mass bewilderment in a symbolic city as we see in the last part of *The Possessed*, and it is to Dostoyevsky we must turn in order to see, by comparison, how unreal the characterization is of Gogol's little monsters compared to Dostoyevsky's more orthodox technique.

A word must be said about the famous lyrical digressions of Gogol. There is too little time to analyse them in detail, but it would be a mistake to put too much emphasis on their contents. Just as he was fond of juxtaposing incongruous words and concepts, he had also a taste for the bizarre conjunction of styles. He played like an organist on the stops of pathos, exuberance, pure poetic lyricism and the tones of chatty conversation. He liked nothing better than to send a reader crashing from the heights of lyricism to the depths of the banal. In Chapter 11 we have a lyrical gust, as Chichikov is speeding along in his troika:

> Russia, Russia, I see you from afar . . . and your mighty expanse enfolds me, reflected with terrifying force in the depths within me. My eyes are lighted up with supernatural power. Oh, what glittering wondrous infinity of space the world knows nothing of! Oh Russia . . .

The spate of rhetoric is suddenly interrupted by another coach driver cursing Chichikov and requesting the devil to flay his soul if he does not get out of the way.

Apart from this the lyrical digressions provide an emotional contrast, a subtle variation in tone difficult to convey to a reader in translation. But from a purely acoustic standpoint this novel is a tone poem in prose with strange indefinable subtleties of rhythm and melody.

On a more practical level the digressions serve to convey Chichikov from one tableau to another in the episodic construction of the book, and serve to waft him out of the narrative altogether, on the wings of a lyrical spate which compares Russia to a troika.

It must also be taken into consideration that Gogol suffered from verbal diarrhoea and literally liked the sound of his own voice. He was a great, an accomplished reader of his own works.

What then is the point of *Dead Souls* if we insist on looking for one? It lies in two things: Gogol's artistic instincts and his religious views. His artistic instinct was for the comically absurd, and he had a virtually irrepressible genius for the creation of the squalid non-humans in which his work abounds. As one of his contemporaries observed, Gogol's artistic imagination could seize upon an anecdote or a detail and create a wildly fantastic embroidering of a theme. Unfortunately, from his childhood, Gogol had inculcated into him by his mother a strong moral sense largely based on an unhealthy fear of the Devil. One does not wish now to sound like the critics who see the Devil lurking behind every comma of Gogol, but it is a biographical and literary fact. In his other works we see a progressive change in Gogol's attitude towards the Devil. His early stories are full of little demons, friendly fellows for the most part, who play cards with humans and can easily be kept at bay, if objectionable, by a prayer. As time goes on these little devils become more and more sinister until finally we see in 1835 the horror story *Viy* in which the devils assume horrible proportions and have absolute dominion over men.

After this, and during the writing of *Dead Souls*, Gogol's religious views in the soil of his sick mind grew into nasty plants. He confused artistic and moral criteria and reached the conclusion that an artistically good author produces morally good characters. Unfortunately, Gogol's own artistic talents stretched only as far as depicting mediocre non-humans, a state of affairs Gogol attributed to his own sinfulness. While writing *Dead Souls* he staved off the crisis by promising himself that he would depict the sins of Chichikov in the first volume, the work we have now. A second volume would show Chichikov redeemed. This is the meaning of all those hints in the last chapter about man falling on his knees in the dust before the heavens. It seems that Gogol was trying to create his own squalid divine comedy and bring Chichikov from the Hell of his misdeeds to the Paradise of redemption.

In adopting this attitude, Gogol was continuing a Russian tradition which had always stressed the moral importance of literature. Karamzin had declared at the beginning of the century that a good author should be a virtuous man[1] and it was Gogol's unstable mind that gave this axiom such terrible consequences for his art. The preaching of virtue in Russian literature had usually two applications. Some authors, like Karamzin and Gogol, saw it in terms of personal reform, others, such as Radischev and critics of the sixties, saw it in political or social terms, but the same urge to moralize and to reform inspires them all. In his last much abused book, *Selected Passages from a Correspondence with Friends*, Gogol preaches brotherly love, the submission of all classes to religion as exemplified by the Russian Church and the general cultivation of personal virtue. It is easy to mock the extravagance of Gogol's tone, but it should be remembered that these opinions, for which Gogol

---

[1] N. M. Karamzin: *Izbrannyye sochineniya* (Moscow-Leningrad 1964, 2 vols.), Vol. I, p. 122. 'I am certain,' writes Karamzin, 'that a bad man cannot be a good author'.

has been universally condemned, are the very same which Dosto-
evsky incorporated into his novels and for which he receives
virtually universal acclaim.[1]

It is often difficult for critics with a bent for social reform to
appreciate that it is possible to be indignant at moral evils while
still supporting the political system under which they flourish. All
the biographical and textual evidence indicates that Gogol was
such a man. His novel is a moral, not a social, satire. The faults and
sins which he attacks are universal. Plyushkin's miserliness is not a
consequence of the feudal system, but yet another manifestation
of a sin common to many people in any epoch. The same can be
said of Manilov's saccharine ineffectualness and Nozdryov's
bullying. They are all human types which, in *real life*, as Dosto-
evsky observes, are only seen in diluted form.[2]

All the traditional picaresque novels have a streak of moralizing
in them, usually expressed by the reform of the hero. Chichikov
was to be redeemed in three stages. Part one of the novel, which we
have now considered, was Chichikov in the Inferno, part two was
to see his remorse in Purgatory, part three was to see his regeneration into a New Man. Gogol struggled with his task for years,
having fallen into that fatal confusion of artistic and moral values
which was to destroy him. Round Mr. Chichikov resolutely refused
to be made square. The *good* characters of part two who were to
propel him to penitence are flat and unconvincing, whereas the
few monsters which slipped out of Gogol's pen are as alive and
amusing as those in part one. Attributing this state of affairs to his
own sinfulness, Gogol found that Mr. Chichikov was beyond
redemption and so, Gogol thought, was Gogol. We see from
Selected Passages that Chichikov's reform was essentially religious
and the reform of society, if Gogol ever thought of it, was in
terms of personal morality, leaving untouched the social evils

[1] Professor Zeldin in the introduction to his recent translation of *Selected Passages*
has rightly called for a reassessment of Gogol's views as expressed in the book,
hitherto dismissed as the reactionary aberrations of a madman (*Nikolai Gogol:
Selected Passages from a Correspondence with Friends*, trans. and intro. by Jesse Zeldin
(Vanderbilt U.P., Nashville 1969)).
[2] See Dostoyevsky's discourse on Gogol's characters, *The Idiot*, Part IV, Chapter I.
Setchkarev expresses the nature of Gogol's art aptly and succinctly: 'All realism
was alien to Gogol. In ever increasing measure he concerned himself with something far more essential' (V. Setchkarev: *Gogol: his life and works* (London 1968)),
p. 187.

such as serfdom, which Gogol's admirers thought he was attacking.

Dead Souls is a sort of inferno in which Gogol mocked all he considered diabolical in life; self-centred mediocrity, bad taste, preoccupation with trivia and all the moral evils which the Russians sum up in a superbly untranslatable word *poshlost'*. Had we a word for it, we might apply it to people who like plastic gnomes, who like everything *nice* and who fill their rooms with what they consider to be trendy examples of modern art, not because they like the stuff but because they are up and coming in the world and have to show a sense of awareness to contemporary trends of thought. *Poshlost'* cannot actually be pinned down to definite external phenomena because it is essentially a moral defect which assumes different forms in different people at different times. It can best be defined as the bogus and the phoney passing themselves off as genuine but doing it so cleverly, and with such a fanfare, that they often pass unnoticed. It is the technique of erecting a façade to conceal decay and ugliness.

One suspects that there was a large streak of *poshlost'* running through Gogol because he portrays these people with a zeal which amounts almost to affection. The smoothness of Chichikov in part one is so lovingly portrayed that there seems to be a love-hate relationship between him and Gogol and it is as much Gogol's guilty conscience as anything else which urges Chichikov towards repentance in part two.

Unable to express and portray his dislike of this cosmic mediocrity in terms of genuine human life, Gogol had recourse to the transmutation of external phenomena into something like symbols. Trivialities of action and behaviour are related in tones of august solemnity and Mr. Chichikov, this so nice, so charming, so adaptable man, rolls relentlessly on through his world of melons, cucumbers and pumpkins in order to find means of feathering his round little nest. We meet a descendant of him in *The Brothers Karamazov*, the snotty-nosed little devil with a cold in his head who torments Ivan. Chichikov moves in an inferno of Gogol's invention but as we have observed, there is something of the Homeric here too. The similes, the frequent feasting and the epic structure of the novel make Chichikov a bogus Odysseus, but there is no place for him in either Paradise or Ithaca. And besides, it would have been totally beyond Gogol's abilities to portray Penelope or Beatrice.

Chichikov is a picaresque hero, on the move and on the make, journeying through a moral, not a social hell. One can finally call *Dead Souls* a picaresque Odyssey through the inferno and, having satisfied the critic's biological urge to categorize, leave it at that.

BIBLIOGRAPHY

Texts

GOGOL, NIKOLAI: *Dead Souls*, trans. David Magarshack (Penguin Books, Harmondsworth 1969).
— *Dead Souls*, trans. Constance Garnett (London 1922), 2 vols.
— *Letters of Nikolai Gogol*, selected, ed. and trans. Karl F. Proffer (Ann Arbor 1967).

Critical Works

GOGOL, Nikolai:
Debreczeny, Paul: 'Nikolai Gogol and his Contemporary Critics', *Transactions of the American Philosophical Society* (Philadelphia, April 1966).
Erlich, Victor: *Gogol* (Yale U.P., New York and London 1969).
Lavrin, Janko: *Gogol* (London 1925).
Magarshack, D.: *Gogol, a life* (London 1957).
Mirsky, D. S.: *A History of Russian Literature*, ed. and abridged by Francis J. Whitfield (New York 1960), pp. 143–55.
Nabokov, Vladimir: *Nikolai Gogol* (Norfolk, Conn. 1944).
Setchkarev, V.: *Gogol, his life and works* (London 1968).
Slomimsky, A.: *Tekhnika Komicheskogo u Gogolya* (Petrograd 1923).
Stepanov, N.: *N. Gogol' Tvorcheskiy Put'* (Moscow 1955).

INDEX